1

PERSPECTIVES ON AGING
AND HUMAN DEVELOPMENT Series

BEING AND
BECOMING OLD

EDITOR: JON HENDRICKS

Baywood Publishing Company, Inc.

Library of Congress Catalog Card Number: 79-65154
ISBN Number: 0-89503-014-4

Library of Congress Cataloging in Publication Data
Main entry under title:

Being and becoming old.

    (Perspectives on aging and human development
series ; 1)
    Includes bibliographical references.
    1. Aged--Psychology--Addresses, essays, lectures.
2. Aging--Psychological aspects--Addresses, essays,
lectures. 3. Self-perception--Addresses, essays, lectures. 4. Life cycle, Human--Addresses, essays,
lectures. I. Hendricks, Jon, 1943-   II. Series.
HQ1061.B415   301.43'5   79-65154
ISBN 0-89503-014-4

preface

The study of aging has been thoroughly enriched by the contributions of its social psychologists. So pervasive has their influence become that the claim that all social gerontologists are to some extent social psychologists has been made more than once. Most obvious among the many insights furnished by such a perspective is the need to focus on the interactive effects operating between the current state of one's intrapersonal affairs, his or her biographical circumstances and those contextual factors which impinge on his or her life-world. Indeed, even so fundamental a contention as *age differences* versus *age changes*, now taken for granted by students of the aging process, is a fairly recent addition wrought from the work of our social psychologically oriented brethren. Any attempt to enumerate the specific benefits of such a point of view might run on *ad nauseam;* suffice it to say that such a model is aimed at an articulation of the ways in which individuals moving through the life course affect and are in turn affected by their social surroundings. Quite clearly, the boundaries of a social psychological perspective are maddeningly broad, but perhaps this is its strength as well.

The articles collected here, originally published in the *International Journal of Aging and Human Development*, exemplify the best of the social psychological literature in the field of gerontology. What they do not represent, however, is a unitary point of view. To have selected them to that end would have been contrary to the best interest of scholary development. Instead the various essays in each of the three subsections are intended to portray the diversity of alternative foci within a social psychological perspective. They are didactic in the hope that they will point the way to the formulation of new models capable of spelling out in even clearer detail the relationship between personal growth and societal change. One of the surest ways of forging tomorrow's paradigms is through a juxtaposition of today's most resourceful conceptualizations.

Part I is comprised of three conceptual choices. Despite their eclecticism, all insist on an appreciation of the individual actor's intentional consciousness. Lowenthal points out that the extent to which persons adjust to their changing life circumstances is dependent on the congruence between their behavior and their personal expectations. While many aspects of Lowenthal's argument parallel what is often referred to as phenomenology, Marshall's piece reflects another of the current trends in social psychology—that of symbolic interactionism. Adopting the metaphor of a career, Marshall maintains that passage into old age is unique among life's transitions as it has no exit. Consequently, gerontologists must attend to the ways in which individuals attempt to control a reality over which they have largely relinquished their priority. Lieberman provides a critical examination of the whole issue of adaptation, concluding that personality factors outweigh contextual inputs among the three ethnic groups he studied. While many will quarrel with the merits of such a claim, Lieberman does sensitize us to the need to carefully consider common features of the human condition.

Having established some of the conceptual parameters of a social psychological perspective, Part II turns its attention to the question of alterations in self-perception over the life course, especially how objective and subjective definitions are interwoven. Back reminds the reader that role change among the elderly should not be construed as role loss, rather, an event's personal meaning must be ascertained before such an assessment is made. First Rose, then Kastenbaum and his colleagues provide refinements of the ways in which various components of one's life world affect how old people seem to themselves. Quite obviously the passing of the calendar is not in itself a totally accurate construct for judging age. Finally, Lawrence elevates a similar set of issues and the manner in which the perceived age of a new acquaintance colors subsequent expectations.

The three selections in Part III focus on the coping skills manifested in the middle years and beyond. Reporting on data derived from a forty year longitudinal study, Kuypers notes the role played by early life antecedents in determining adaptibility in the later years. Interestingly enough, long standing patterns vary not only by intellectual capabilities, social status, appropriate models in use but by sex as well. Livson provides additional insight into personality differences in two groups of middle aged women drawn from the Berkeley longitudinal panel. Labelling her two groups traditional or independent, Livson provides a wealth of information concerning corollaries which emerge in their health and well-being. Concentrating on male respondents in the Normal Aging Study of the Veterans Administration, Costa and McCrae underscore the importance of flexible sex-role identification in later life if maximal satisfaction is to be maintained.

All of the essays, each in its own way, speak to the interaction between people and social environment. A number of cross-cutting themes become increasingly apparent as one reads the various selections, but the effect is additive. From here the reader should be prepared to offer a renewed challenge and a new contribution to the growing social psychological resources of the field. This is hardly the first step, yet neither will it be the last.

table of contents

PART THREE – PERSONALITY: CHANGE AND CONTINUITY OVER THE LIFE COURSE

part one

SOCIAL-PSYCHOLOGICAL
PERSPECTIVES
OF THE AGING PROCESS

chapter 1

INTENTIONALITY: TOWARD A FRAMEWORK FOR THE STUDY OF ADAPTATION IN ADULTHOOD

Marjorie Fiske Lowenthal

The hypothesis proposed in this paper is that a significant component of the adaptive process in adult life consists of the individual's efforts to achieve, restore, or maintain some yet to be determined degree of congruence or equilibrium between his conscious goals and his behavioral pattern. Corollaries to this hypothesis are that certain features of the individual's social networks, his perceptions of these networks, his characteristic modes of perceiving stress, and his time perspective are crucial predisposing and intervening variables in accounting for modes of adjustment between intentions and behavior. The paradigm also provides for systematic exploration of the important question of the relationship between global goals (or values) and concrete goals, and the comparative importance for adaptation of the congruence of each with behavior.

It is not assumed that maintaining some degree of goodness of fit between ends and means is the only process accounting for development and change in adult life, nor that it is of equal importance in all levels of society, nor in all cultures. We agree with Maddox (1970) that what is most needed now in the study of adult change is not a global theory but a number of alternative paradigms which take into account both sociological and psychological models and concepts.[1] The model presented here hopefully comprises a small step toward a more comprehensive body of an adult developmental theory. In its emphasis on conscious goals, as well as in its concern with the individual's perceptions of his social networks as critical intervening variables, this framework is related to the cognitive theory of personality change in adulthood as recently proposed by Thomae (1970). In reference to Riegel's (1969) recent review of developmental models, it falls between the "jig-saw puzzle" and "developmental stage" types. The model proposed here differs from both of these, however, in that it provides for the study of homeostasis or retrogression as well as growth. It is currently being applied to a longitudinal study of transitional stages in adult life;[2] illustrations will be drawn largely from the baseline data of that study.

[1] This paper further develops concepts tentatively sketched in Lowenthal, M. F. (in press) and in Lowenthal, M. F., Spence, D., Thurnher, M. (in press). The critical encouragement of Professor Rosow in this development has been indispensable. The author is also grateful to Professor Margaret Clark for her pertinent suggestions.
[2] NICHD HD 03051. The study is being conducted by the Adult Development Program at Langley Porter Institute, University of California, San Francisco.

BACKGROUND

There is, of course, nothing new about the significance of conscious intentions, as contrasted with instincts and unconscious needs, in the study of adulthood. On the broadest level, the framework proposed here builds on the concept of Murray (1962), that a relatively few number of "ends which are desired for their own sake" can be ascribed to most individuals. Allport (1961) offers a similar thesis, although he uses such terms as "cardinal dispositions" or "intentions" rather than "ends." Influenced by this tradition, White (1960, 1961) places more emphasis on means than on particular ends, suggesting that the sense of competence or effectance should be added to man's basic needs. Bühler (1968) has developed a typology of needs, which may be conscious or not, derived in part from a study of life goals. While they differ in emphasis and direction, these works suggest that most adults have broad aims or objectives, and that they are definable and few.

The assumption that conscious reappraisal of goals is a significant part of the adaptive process in the course of the adult life cycle resembles Butler's (1963) concept of the "life review" as a prerequisite to psychic equilibrium in old age. In a recent work, Erikson (1969, p. 438) points to "man's basic need to confess the past in order to purge it," perhaps an essential step to the achievement of ego integrity which he postulates as the major developmental task of mature age (Erikson, 1950, 1959). Erikson and Butler, however, true to their psychoanalytic orientations, stress the importance for adaptation of the review process itself, in the abstract, as it were. The model proposed here focuses on the consequences of this process for change in the individual's global values and concrete goals, and his goal-related behavior.

There are very few studies of developmental changes in goals, nor are there many cross-sectional studies which would lend themselves to developmental or generational comparisons. The majority, as reflected in the work of Caro (1966), Rosenberg (1957), and Kilby (1965), have studied mainly the occupational aspirations of high school or college students. Seldom has research been directed toward determining the goals of middle-aged and elderly populations. Exceptions include Chinoy's (1955) study of automobile workers, which traces differences in the definition of "success" between young and older workers. Reichard, et al. (1962), in a study of styles of aging derived from clusters of personality characteristics, conclude that: " . . . aging may itself lead to a renunciation of unattained goals and so to a reduction in experienced frustration . . . consistent with our hypothesis that disappointments lose potency in retrospect if hopeless goals are renounced." Kuhlen (1956) suggests that there may be an age-trend toward greater specificity of goals. Studying a cross-section of age groups, Kornhauser (1965) reports that "purposeful striving" is highly correlated with the mental health status of the industrial worker, but that purposiveness in work is related to positive mental health among young workers, while purposiveness in nonwork activities is more significant among the middle-aged. The model proposed in this paper goes one step further and postulates that congruence between purposiveness, or goals, and the behavioral pattern is itself an indicator of adaptation.

While emphasizing the goodness of fit between goals and behavior, the model also provides for an examination of the congruence between global goals or values, those which the individual postulates as his general guidelines for living, and concrete goals, which may be short or long range. In exploring the latter type of consonance, we shall in effect be comparing what Smith (1969) calls superego-required values with self-required values. In exploring the balance between goals and behavioral patterns, we shall also be pursuing a task which Smith proposes is one of the most urgent needs in behavioral science today: the study of the behavioral implications of values. In so doing, our approach differs somewhat from that of Rosow (1965) who develops a four-fold typology of socialization based on the adoption or lack of adoption of socially sanctioned values and behavior. He has called these types the socialized, the dilettante, the chameleon and the unsocialized. His concern with commitment and behavior in terms of expectations crucial for the social system differs somewhat from the schema proposed in this paper, which is based on commitments which may or may not reflect the system's basic values. As will become apparent later, however, once the goals-behavior constellations have been established, some will lend themselves to arrangement within the Rosow typology.

In providing a framework for tracing the relationship between goals and social networks and perceptions, as well as between goals and other characteristics of the self, the model herein proposed may be viewed as a step toward examining the discouragingly complex problems of the articulation between personal and social systems in a limited but potentially manageable fashion, a step encouraged by sociological and developmental theorists alike. Parsons (1949), for example, starting with an initial focus on the significance of social networks and styles of interpersonal relationships in the action system of an individual, noted in his early formulations that this constellation must be related to the individual's ultimate ends. His subsequent elaborations of the interrelationship between personal and social systems (e.g., 1956, 1963) form a backdrop for theories of the middle-range, such as those of Merton (1957) and Hyman (1960), bearing on the significance of reference groups and reference individuals in the development of the individual's values and intentions. The proposed framework, with such referents postulated as predisposing and intervening influences on the goals-behavior constellation, provides one kind of response to Merton's plea for more empirical study of the process of self-selection of reference groups, and the relation between such selection and self-appraisal. It should also enable us to distinguish between processes that have been defined as: primary socialization, those by which the individual takes on his principal value orientations (Inkeles, 1968; Clausen, 1968); secondary or adult socialization, the process by which he moves through normative role changes without change in basic values (Brim, 1968; Berger and Luckmann, 1966); and alternation, the process of dramatic conversion-like change involving value reorientations (Berger, 1963; Berger and Luckmann, 1966; Boulding, 1966).

As the leading exponents of the need for data and theory in adult development point out (Birren, 1964; Clausen, in press; Havighurst, 1961a, 1961b; Kuhlen, 1964; Neugarten, 1964, 1966, in press; Neugarten, et al., 1964; Pressey and Kuhlen, 1957), there is as yet a relatively small body of research, either longitudinal or cross-sectional, specifically designed to study the interrelationship between socializing agents and factors and the psychological aspects of adult development. This in part results from early psychoanalytic influences which tended to view the individual as definitively formed primarily by the circumstances of his infancy and early childhood. It is not accidental that a considerable proportion of the research on adulthood done thus far is based on samples, now adult, originally drawn for studies of early personality development in children. In studying change in these groups in later life, the emphasis is, perforce, on those characteristics selected for the study of childhood, with consequent relative neglect of adult socialization processes (e.g., see Clausen, 1964).

In the work of Neugarten (1969, in press), personality changes in adulthood are indeed examined in the light of factors associated with processes of socialization, such as age norms and age constraints. Conversely, disengagement theory (Cumming and Henry, 1961), which postulates a highly compatible change in the individual's relationship to his society and in his society's relationship to him with advancing age, is now being examined in the light of self-concept and personality constructs (Henry, 1964, 1965; Havighurst, Neugarten, and Tobin, 1964; Williams and Wirths, 1965; Cumming, 1968). The model proposed in this paper focuses on perceptions of the self and perceptions of reference individuals, groups and norms in relation to goal formulation and change. This model should provide a framework for making at least tentative distinctions between changes attributable to innate or developmental factors and those resulting from social processes and pressures.

Finally, this model has also evolved in part from earlier research on studies of normal and abnormal aging.[3] This work suggested the importance of conscious reappraisal and often reorientation of goals and of goal-related behavior in order to achieve some degree of equilibrium between the two domains (Clark and Anderson, 1967; Lowenthal, et al., 1967). For the older subjects studied in this research, this reorientation typically took one of three forms: (*a*) renouncing goals which for reasons of social constraint or physiological limitations were no longer feasible, sometimes substituting practicable goals relating to the same global values or overall intentions; (*b*) reevaluating or reinterpreting past choices and behavior in such a way that they emerge as compatible with global values; or (*c*) shifting the behavioral pattern away from the concrete goals of middle age and toward the previously obscured or overlaid values and aspirations of adolescence and young adulthood.

The retrospective reports of these elderly respondents also suggested that the individual's characteristic modes of perceiving himself and certain dimensions of his social networks are closely related to the choices he makes in his efforts to reestablish equilibrium between goals and behavior at transitional stages of later life. Among relevant self-perceptions are what might be called a "stress-proneness" dimension, illustrated by two individuals exposed to roughly equivalent levels of life stresses, one of whom dwells on stress in recounting his life history, whereas the other merely recounts it and goes on to other matters. Among social perceptions that seem relevant to the capacity for making adjustments between goals and behavior are the individual's views of his close, intermediate, and remote social networks as hostile or benign.

THE MODEL

To recapitulate, the overall purpose of the framework herewith proposed is to test the hypothesis that adjustment between goals and goal-related behavior patterns constitutes a significant adaptive process in adulthood. More specifically, the objective of the model is to provide a framework to:

a. examine the relationship between global values and concrete goals at selected stages of adult life;

[3] NIMH 09145

b. trace changes in the nature and direction of the individual's global and concrete goals;

c. explore the relationship between global and concrete goals on the one hand and goal-related behavior on the other;

d. determine whether transitions in adult life which are customarily viewed as incremental (involving role gain such as going to college, acquiring a first job, marriage, parenthood) foster growth-promoting processes in the ensuing adjustment between intentions and behavior; and

e. determine whether transitions normatively viewed as decremental (involving role loss such as the empty nest or retirement)[4] foster homeostatic, retrogressive, or growth-inhibiting processes of adjustment between the two domains of intentions and behavior. In addition, we shall compare changes in the goals-behavior constellation among persons who did and did not undergo a normative transition. We will then compare these two groups with persons undergoing idiosyncratic or unscheduled transitions such as divorce, bereavement, major occupational shifts, and chronic illness. The objective of such comparisons is to determine whether trends toward growth, homeostasis, or retrogression are usually associated with transitions, or whether they also take place in their absence.

Before describing how these objectives will be pursued, a note is in order about the study currently testing the model, which requires data on the same subjects at two points in time. In this research, called the "transitions study," two groups of subjects at the first point of contact face transitions normatively viewed as incremental, and two face those normatively viewed as decremental. Subjects likely to undergo an incremental transition include high school seniors facing college, first job, or marriage, and newlyweds, among whom at least half can be expected to have a child within four years. Those facing transitions usually viewed as decremental include parents whose youngest child is a senior in high school (who are, in other words, facing the empty-nest or post-parental stage), and subjects anticipating retirement, at least half of whom can be expected to retire before the projected four-year follow-up. Within each group, half are men, half women. Altogether, there are 218 intensively studied subjects. In the interest of reducing analytic complexity as much as possible, socioeconomic status is limited to the middle and lower middle class economically (about half each blue-collar and white-collar workers), and ethnically primarily to Anglo-Americans. At the time of the four-year follow-up, new cohorts of high school seniors and middle-aged parents will be added to the sample according to the Schaie design (Schaie, 1965, 1967). The purpose of these new samples is to provide some basis for differentiating between historical trends and developmental change.

The characterization of transitional stages as incremental or decremental is, as has been noted, normative. The incremental transitions, involving role gain, impose a new set of more or less prescribed behaviors and are generally viewed as growth-promoting and favorable for the individual. A decremental transition, such as retirement, usually involves role loss, frequently requires the elimination of a prescribed set of behaviors, is often

---

[4] These normative views involve value judgments: incremental transitions tend to be seen as gains for the individual, decremental as losses. These views are of course not universally shared. An incremental transition such as marriage may in some instances be anticipated (or experienced) as a loss, while a decremental one may be construed as a gain. Variations in perception of the pending transition constitute a dimension of the analytic framework.

children?

negatively viewed, and is considered unfortunate or unpleasant for the individual. In general, incremental transitions tend to be voluntary, whereas decremental transitions are often involuntary.

To take first a brief overview of the analytic sequence, at time one, independent variables such as sex, life stage, and socioeconomic status will be examined in relation to the experimental variables, which consist of the nature of goals and the congruence between goals and behavior; goals-behavior congruence will in turn be examined for each stage/sex group in relation to indicators of adaptation (validating variables). When follow-up data become available, the experimental variables of baseline goals and the congruence between goals and behavior become antecedent, whereas the goals-behavior configurations at the time of follow-up will be outcome variables. As noted earlier, prior research in the Adult Development Program has isolated certain social and psychological characteristics that appear to play a significant role in adult adaptation. These characteristics will be examined as predisposing variables at time one, and the change in them, between times one and two, will become intervening variables in the analysis of time two data. The usefulness of the concept that changes in the relationship between goals and behavior are a crucial mode of adaptation in adulthood will be tested by comparing the various goals-behavior outcomes with the change in a number of more conventional indicators of adaptation, which at time two continue to be validating variables.

Table 1 presents the model for two points in time.

EXPLICATION OF THE MODEL

In further describing this framework, some of the less evident dimensions of each column will be briefly defined, followed by a more detailed elaboration of the analytic sequence, illustrated with one dimension from each column.

Turning first to the experimental variables (columns A-3 and B-2), dimensions of goals and behavior include content, such as expressive/instrumental; and structural, such as expansive/restrictive. Both global and concrete goals will be analyzed in terms of these and related dimensions, which include, from a substantive perspective, such categories as hedonistic, spiritual, and social service; from a structural perspective, futurity and variety. Global or overarching goals, which might properly be termed values, are derived from a different set of questions than the concrete, often short term aims; they will be compared with specific aims, and the degree of congruence will be determined. Overarching and specific goals will then be assessed respectively for goodness of fit, or congruence with behavior. This will provide a basis for testing Kuhlen's (1964) hypothesis that concrete goals become increasingly relevant to adaptation in later life. It will also allow for the testing of the hypothesis, growing out of earlier research in the Adult Development Program, that past concrete goals are often reevaluated and redefined to bring about a better fit with global goals. This procedure also will permit exploration of the comparative importance for adaptation, at different life stages, of the congruence between global goals and behavior, and concrete goals and behavior. The degree of congruence measured through such analyses may or may not prove to have predictive value for goodness of fit at time two, after the intervening transition has taken place.

The predisposing variables (column A-2), and the change in them between times one and two when they become intervening variables (column B-2b), are expected to have

TABLE 1
Model for Study of Transitions

A. Time One

(1) Independent Variables	(2) Predisposing Variables	(3) Experimental Variables	(4) Validating Variables
Sex SES Life stage (etc.)	Stress Stress perception Social networks Social perceptions Time perspective Perceptions of the pending transition†	Congruence between global and concrete goals Congruence between global goals and behavior* Congruence between concrete goals and behavior	Life satisfaction Self-concept Level of functioning Degree of psychological impairment Anxiety level

B. Time Two

(1) Experimental Variables	(2) Intervening Variables		(3) Outcome Variables	(4) Validating Variables (changes in)
	(2a) Transitions	(2b) Time Two		
Time one congruence global/concrete goals Time one congruence goals/behavior	Incremental Decremental None	Stress Stress perception Social networks Social perception Time perspective	Time two congruence global/concrete goals Time two congruence goals/behavior*	Life satisfaction Self-concept Level of functioning Degree of impairment Anxiety level

*Selected dimensions, e.g., expressive/instrumental; expansive/constrictive.
† E.g., voluntary/involuntary; positive/negative.

9

considerable explanatory power in accounting for the goals-behavior constellation. Subjective perceptions are to be examined in the light of objective indicators. For example, the individual's perceptions of the nature of his interpersonal relationships (Lowenthal and Haven, 1968) and of his extrapersonal social networks will be assessed, as well as behavioral patterns reflecting the depth and scope of his social interactions. Similarly, not only will indicators of presumed stress be developed, but also a dimension of preoccupation with stress. Typologies of time perspective, or sense of futurity, will take into account age and health status, or a kind of actuarial life-expectancy. Perception of future time is expected to be associated with the nature of adjustments made in goals and behavior during a transition. Finally, the perception of a pending transition as voluntary or involuntary, welcome or unwelcome, is also expected to influence the nature of the adjustments made to it between times one and two.

In order to test the hypothesis, which states that the attainment or maintenance of some degree of congruity between goals and behavior is a critical adaptive process in adult transitions, we will compare goals-behavior congruence before and after the transitions with conventional indicators of adaption (validating variables, column A-4 and B-4). These indicators include measures of impairment, anxiety, level of functioning, mood, satisfaction, and self-concept. They are derived from scales, symptoms lists, self-ratings, global ratings by an interdisciplinary team, and projective data.

In the following sections, the interrelationship of the broad domains of the model will be further developed from selected dimensions of the various columns, together with correlative hypotheses and research questions.

The Goal-Behavior Constellation: Structural Dimension[5]

The degree of congruence between goals and behavior will, as mentioned above, be measured along several structural and substantive dimensions. Earlier research, as well as preliminary analyses of the time one data on the transitions study, suggest that an instrumental/expressive continuum may be the most common among the substantive dimensions and an expansive/constrictive one among the structural. These dimensions derive from the goal domain, and will be applied to the behavioral as well. In the interest of simplicity, the exposition here will be largely limited to the expansive/constrictive (structural) dimension. Table 2 illustrates the typology to be derived from this dimension as applied to goals and behavior. (The table somewhat oversimplifies the analytic process; in actuality the expansive/constrictive dimension will consist of at least two components, one of scope or breadth, the other of intensity, depth, or complexity.)

Cells 1 and 4 represent good fit or equilibrium between goals and behavior: cell 1 reflects homeostatic or retrogressive tendencies, cell 4 growth-promoting tendencies. Cells 2 and 3 reflect two types of poor fit or incongruence. There may be more tolerance for incongruence at certain periods of life than others; for example, many high school seniors who rank high on conventional indicators of adaptation fall in cell 2. In general, however, incongruence sustained from time one to time two is expected to be associated with other indicators of maladaption.

A transition, as used here, imposes behavioral change, the addition of a new set of activities in an incremental transition, and the dropping of a set of activities in a decremental one. Turning first to a consideration of outcome in the goals-behavior constellation for the individuals in the four cells of Table 2, it is obvious that some

[5] Column A-3, Table 1.

persons will gain improved equilibrium, others will be thrown out of balance, if they merely follow the path of least resistance and adopt the behavioral pattern imposed by the transition.

Consequences of Simple Conformity to Imposed Behavioral Change

When an individual with expansive preexisting goals and restricted behavior at time one (cell 2, Table 2) undergoes an incremental transition (e.g., becoming a college student, marriage, first job), congruence at time two may result without his making any change in his goals, simply by adopting the expected behavior. A decremental transition (departure of a child from home or retirement) may result in congruence if the previous goals were more constricted than behavior (as in cell 3), either in anticipation of the new stage, or because they had been restricted all along. Persons likely to be thrown off balance by adopting the expected behavior are those with constricted equilibrium facing an incremental transition, and those with an expansive equilibrium who face a decremental one. Table 3, then, illustrates the goals-behavior constellations which would prevail with the advent of a transition if individuals in the four cells of Table 2 did nothing but conform to the expanded or constricted behavior required by the transition.

Cells 3 and 8 represent those for whom the expanded or restricted behavior imposed by the transition would improve the congruence between goals and behavior. Our data suggest that in many instances the goals at time one may already be restricted in anticipation of a decremental transition, and expanded in anticipation of an incremental

TABLE 2
Goals-Behavior Constellation
(Column A-3, B-3, Table 1, structural dimension)

	Behavior	
Goals or Intentions	Constricted (−)	Expansive (+)
Constricted (−)	(1) − −	(3) − +
Expansive (+)	(2) + −	(4) + +

TABLE 3
Potential Consequences of Adopting Behavior Expected
in Two Types of Transitions

	Type of Transition (Column B-2a, Table 1)	
Time One Goals-Behavior Relationship (Column A-3, Table 1)	Incremental	Decremental
Congruence (equilibrium)		
Constricted, both domains (Cell 1, Table 2)	(1) Incongruence	(5) Congruence
Expansive, both domains (Cell 4, Table 2)	(2) Congruence	(6) Incongruence
Incongruence (disequilibrium)		
Expansive goals, constricted behavior (Cell 2, Table 2)	(3) Congruence	(7) Incongruence
Constricted goals, expansive behavior (Cell 3, Table 2)	(4) Incongruence	(8) Congruence

one. Persons in cells 3 and 8 may, if such anticipatory self-socialization proves to be prevalent, represent modal types. For example, the preretirement male may, in anticipation of retirement, have restricted his occupational goals and established goals of ease and pleasure; thus when he actually retires, the elimination of the work role will bring about equilibrium between his goals and his behavior. Cells 4 and 7 represent those who would remain in disequilibrium or exacerbated disequilibrium at the onset of a transition if they do not alter their goals, because the imposed change in behavior is the opposite of what would be required to bring about congruence with the pretransition goals. If they should rank fairly high on the validating adaptation variables at times one and two, these may prove to be persons for whom goals have low salience; for whom a pleasurable or protective pattern of day-to-day behavior is in fact an end in itself.

Among persons whose goals and behavior were compatible on this expansive/constrictive dimension prior to the transition, those constricted in both areas might well remain in comparative equilibrium in a decremental transition (cell 5). Similarly, those who had established an expansive level of congruence and face an incremental transition would be expected to remain in equilibrium without major adjustment of goals (cell 2). It is cells 1 and 6 that are most likely to include persons for whom the transition imposes a serious threat. If they merely conform to the expected expansion or restriction in behavioral style, they will be in a state of disequilibrium to which they are not accustomed. Those in cell 1 might be said to be conforming ritualistically, those in cell 6, reluctantly. An example of the ritualistic conformist would be the new mother who goes through the motions of child care without providing love or nurturance. An example of the reluctant conformist is the hard-driving executive who adopts a seemingly relaxed lifestyle after retirement but retains his need for dominance and control, which he may transfer to his wife or adult children. While we plan to analyze all types of time one to time two change in the goals-behavior constellation, further explication of the model will here be limited to the two groups for whom a transition seems most likely to constitute a threat: the constricted in both domains who face an incremental transition, and the expansive who face a decremental one.

Alternative Change Processes

Thus far, the discussion has centered on how the two types of transition would influence the goals-behavior constellation if the newly imposed behavioral change were adopted and no change made in goals. In considering alternatives to simple behavioral conformity, we are confronted with many logical possibilities, ranging from a radical expansion of both goals and behavior to a radical restriction of both. Some of these processes will result in equilibrium between the two domains at a higher or lower level than prevailed before; others will result in a new disequilibrium. The following table shows how four alternatives for change (other than the ritualistic and reluctant conformity illustrated in Table 3) would influence the goals-behavior balance at the post-transition period for the restricted in an incremental transition, and the expansive in a decremental one.

The conventionally appropriate modes of establishing a new equilibrium would be for the formerly constricted to expand both goals and behavior in adapting to an incremental transition (A), and for expansive individuals to constrict both goals and behavior in adapting to a decremental transition (F). Since both involve radical changes in goals as

TABLE 4
Other Alternatives for Change in Transitions

Change in the Goals-Behavior Constellation*	Outcomes For:	
	The Constricted, in Incremental Transition	The Expansive, in Decremental Transition
Expand both	A. + Congruence: growth	E. + Congruence: transcendence
Constrict both	B. − Congruence: counteraction	F. − Congruence: disengagement
Change goals in expected direction, retain behavior	C. Incongruence: muddling through	G. Incongruence: escapism
Change neither	D. − Congruence: reversion	H. − Congruence: denial

*Since we are dealing with two domains and there is the possibility of expansion, constriction, or no change in each, there are obviously, in addition to the two conformist alternatives already presented in Table 3, two other conceivable alternatives, representing opposing trends in the two domains, i.e., expanding goals while contracting behavior, and vice versa. While mathematically logical, these alternatives are not psychologically meaningful, and they are therefore deleted from the table.

well as behavior, these "appropriate" modes of growth and disengagement, respectively, will not necessarily be the most common change patterns.

Because of their significance to an understanding of the factors and processes fostering and inhibiting growth and mental health, the most deviant cells are of particular interest: persons who move toward growth or expansion in coping with a decremental transition, and those who move toward constriction or regression in an incremental one. At one extreme, transcendents (E) reorient or augment their goal system and reexpand their behavioral style when confronted with a decremental life stage. An example is a woman who, at the baseline interview, facing both widowhood (her husband was mortally ill) and the empty nest, had developed concrete plans for a new career and embarked on a program of professional training.

At the other extreme, some constricted individuals are totally unable to cope with an incremental transition and in fact are so threatened by it that they even further constrict their goals and behavior, in effect counteracting the transition (B). Extremes of this mode would involve pathological revocation or reconstruction of reality, as in the case of the college freshman who suffers a schizophrenic episode, or the new mother who develops a postpartum psychosis. Somewhat less radical forms of reacting include (among the constricted represented in the middle column) simply the retention or reinstatement of the prior goals and behavioral pattern (D). An example of such reversion is the college student who drops out, or the new mother who neglects her child. The parallel possibility for persons with a prior expansive equilibrium faced with a decremental transition, is the retention of former expansive goals and the attempt to retain a now obsolete behavioral style (H); this amounts, in effect, to a denial of the transition. An example would be the retiree who haunts his former place of employment, or the more extreme instance of a retired stock broker who continued frantically to play the stock market although he no longer had the financial resources to do so.

While the above modes range from the highly creative and adaptive to extremes of maladaptation, they have in common the attainment of equilibrium between goals and behavior, at either a higher or a lower level than prevailed before. In between are two modes of change that result in disequilibrium in the goals-behavior constellation. Cell C (muddling through) involves expansion of goals and retention of the constricted *whole problem of what is a goal—It is a goal different because one activity (way of fulfilling goal) is substituted for another?*

behavioral pattern. This pattern may develop when the incremental transition raises the aspiration level of the individual but imposes behavioral demands beyond his competence, as in some promotions within bureaucracies, amply illustrated in *The Peter Principle* (Peter and Hull, 1969). The remaining alternative, escapism, consists of formerly expansive persons who constrict their goals and perhaps hope to forget them by retaining an expansive behavioral style (G). An example would be the utilities executive in our sample who, many months before his retirement, had already crammed the first year of his postretirement calendar with a lengthy and uninterrupted list of "pleasurable" activities. He explained to the interviewer, "I have this . . . philosophy that once I voluntarily start to slow up, I'll be pushing up the daisies . . . ."

Thus far, congruence and incongruence between goals and behavior have been illustrated, followed by an exploration of how this balance or lack of it would be influenced (a) if the expected behavioral style of a given transition were simply adopted and no goal changes made; and (b) if other logical alternatives for change were pursued. In terms of the basic model (Table 1) we have thus discussed the outcome possibilities (column B-3) for various constellations of the experimental variables (column B-1) on an expansive/constrictive dimension, in the light of the intervening variable of an incremental or decremental transition (column B-2a). Turning next to an illustration of how the predisposing variables (column A-2) will be derived and how (column B-2b) they may be expected to mediate the outcomes depicted in Table 4, all variables will be briefly described, and the stress-perception typology illustrated.

Experiential and Perceptual Modes as Predisposing and Intervening Variables

How does one determine that the perception is not a part of the adaptation rather than a cause?

Perceptions of the transition as positive or negative, voluntary or involuntary, will influence the modes of adapting to it. For example, a student who views his attendance at college as a capitulation to his father's wishes may be most susceptible to a schizophrenic episode; or the girl who has a baby in order to give her mother a much-wanted grandchild may be susceptible to a postpartum psychosis.

At least in the transitions of later life, the individual's sense of personal futurity may also have a bearing on his propensities for expansion or contraction in the goals-behavior constellation. Those with a limited sense of futurity may tend to be the disengagers; those with a broad time extension, the transcendents.

Social behavior (intimate relationships, for example) is also expected to have a bearing *why?* on modes of adaptation to transitions. It may be that growth in the incremental *Dumb!* transition of parenthood is possible only for those who have achieved intimacy in marriage. At the other extreme, escapism after retirement may be the resort of those who have no intimate relationships. Fully as important as the actualities of the individual's social networks is his perception of them. It is likely, for example, that only the clerk with a benign view of his bureaucracy can muddle through in the face of a promotion to executive for which he is ill-equipped. At the other extreme, people with a view of their broader social world as essentially hostile may be prone to resort to denial at retirement.

The final characteristic postulated as a critical predisposing and intervening variable is a composite of actual experience of stressful situations and perceptions of stress. If one envisages a fourfold table with actual stressful events or circumstances (losses,

TABLE 5
Stress Perception
(Columns A-2 and B-2b, Table 1)

Experience of Stress Has Been:	Perception of Stress is:	
	Thematic in Presentation of Self	Not Thematic
Frequent and/or severe	+ + (Overwhelmed)	+ − (Challenged)
Infrequent and/or mild	− + (Anxious)	− − (Lucky)

discontinuities, or other trauma) as one dimension, and the perception of stress as manifest in the presentation of self (in this case, in life history interviews) as the other, four "modes of stress perception" are derived as shown in Table 5.

Groups representing these modes may be provisionally described as the overwhelmed, the defeated, the challenged, and the lucky. The *overwhelmed,* beset by many real losses, bring them up in all sections of the interview; losses, discontinuities and stresses are thematic in their presentation. While there are some young people for whom loss is thematic, this mode, in the natural course of events, tends to be more frequent in the later periods of life because actual losses accumulate. The *anxious,* old or young, on the other hand, have had few losses or discontinuities, but nevertheless their life stories are freighted with a theme of deprivation. They might also be called defeatists. The *challenged,* besieged by many stresses, or a few severe ones, are those who nevertheless do not dwell on them in recounting their histories. It may develop, when the data are analyzed, that this group, in fact, includes a second type—rather than facing and being challenged by stress, some may, in fact, be denying it. Finally, the *lucky* are those who have had few or only mild stresses; loss is not a theme in their protocols, and a few convey the impression of feeling magically protected, chosen, or elect.

In terms of the alternatives for change in the goals-behavior constellation depicted in Table 4, one might conjecture that the overwhelmed may constrict in both realms in the face of any transition, thus counteracting in an incremental one, and disengaging in a decremental one. In light of their presumably low level of personal resources, it may prove to be the anxious who are most likely to be incapable of change in either goals or behavior, reverting to the status quo ante in an incremental transition, while denying a decremental one. The challenged, who presumably have more personal resources, may expand both in goals and behavioral style, growing in an incremental transition, and transcending a decremental one. To the extent that their self-presentation is a camouflage, however, they may turn out also to be deniers in a decremental transition (and thus susceptible, as will be pointed out shortly, to physical or mental illness). The lucky are less clear-cut. Unaccustomed to stress or change, there is little basis for predicting whether they will become overwhelmed, anxious or challenged by a transition; and there are clearly other possibilities. Those who attribute their luck to being chosen or elect may retain their goals and values (so as to continue to seduce whatever fate or deity they conceive as magic helper), but conform to the expected behavior—the ritualistic or reluctant conformists of Table 3. Those who attribute their luck to a kind of magical mastery of their own (Gutmann, 1969), may retain whatever ritualistic behavior to which they attribute their luck (for example, seductiveness or excessive bonhomie), thus muddling through an incremental transition or escaping in a decremental one.

SOCIOPSYCHOLOGICAL IMPLICATIONS

The foregoing explication of the model has been limited primarily to only one structural dimension of the goals-behavior constellation. Equally significant, if not more so, for the study of change in adulthood are the substantive dimensions of global (or values) and concrete goals. As noted, these goal-content dimensions, like the structural ones, are derived from open-ended responses to goal questions and include such categories as instrumental/expressive, growth, ease and contentment, and social commitment. By combining the more frequent structural and content groupings, it should be possible to derive a typology of the more common lifestyles. Two of these, which seem to be fairly clear-cut, are first, what might be called the obsessively instrumental: persons whose commitments as well as behavior are instrumental, and who rank high on expansiveness in both the goal and behavioral domains. A second, rather common, lifestyle consists of persons whose goals and behavior are directed toward comfort or ease, and who tend to be restricted in both domains; this might be called a self-protective lifestyle. If is probable that the lifestyle at time one will prove to have some predictive value for the kinds of adjustments made in adapting to incremental or decremental transitions.

Other questions that may be asked of the data by using the basic model are: (a) whether structural adjustments, such as shifts on the expansive/constrictive continuum, take precedence in a given transition, while substantive shifts, say in an expressive/instrumental dimension, take precedence in another; (b) whether there is a difference between the importance for adaptation of stability vs. change in goals as compared with stability vs. change in behavioral patterns at the various life stages; and (c) whether at some life stages, such as postretirement, stability in behavioral patterns is more closely associated with level of adaptation than is the goodness of fit between goals and behavioral patterns.

The model is also potentially applicable to less scheduled transitions such as parenthood, bereavement, chronic illness, major job changes, and geographic moves. Applied in a fairly long-range longitudinal study for example, it should be useful for studying the process of socialization to parenthood, by comparing change in the goals-behavior constellation before and after the birth of the first, second, and third child, as well as the effects of differing sex distributions among offspring. With more frequent interviews in the pre and postretirement period, the model should contribute to a better understanding of the dynamics of the retirement process, which we suspect has many phases, alternating for a time, perhaps, among stabilizing, retrogressive or growth processes. Applied to studies of various ethnic groups, it could contribute to further understanding of the current cultural clashes in our urban centers. It has long been assumed for example, that expressive goals and behavioral patterns are far more important in some subcultures than others, but that resistance to those instrumental goals which largely characterize Anglo society rarely persists from one generation to another. This assumption has not been explored in depth, however, nor has the possibility that the behavioral style itself may be a major goal in some subcultures, as in at least some groups of blacks in metropolitan areas, or among the Beautiful People for that matter. Applied to higher socioeconomic levels than are currently being studied, and to student activists in comparison with nonactivists, it could also provide a basis for detecting trends in leadership styles, as well as for detecting differences in kind and degree between leaders and nonleaders.

More specifically, as the application of the model proceeds in the current study, it should contribute to further understanding of certain psychosocial processes which in the larger population emerge as major problems. For example in Table 4, those with prior constricted equilibrium who remain constricted in the face of an incremental transition (cell D), may encompass the increasingly high proportion of young people who divorce soon after marriage, drop out soon after entering college, or turn to drugs. If, as we have speculated in connection with the discussion of predisposing or intervening variables, they should turn out to be people who have not yet reached the intimacy stage (in the case of early divorce) or people who are particularly stress prone (in the case of drop-outs), the implications for educational and preventive programs seem fairly clear.

Those who counteract such transitions altogether (cell B, Table 4) may help us to further understand the processes leading to mental illness. If, indeed, these people view the transition as forced upon them, some preventive implications could be readily drawn. Those who retain their expansionist goals but conform to the restricted behavioral style of a decremental transition (cell 6, Table 3), conflicted and frustrated, may develop symptoms of depression between times one and two. Such a finding would help us to explain the dynamics involved in the frequently reported increase in depressive symptoms with advancing age. Similarly, if the escapism and the denial represented in cells G and H in Table 4 prove, as we suspect, to be followed often by physical illness, we may be able to contribute to further understanding of possible psychodynamic factors associated with the increase in illnesses such as strokes and heart attacks, often observed among certain occupational groups after retirement. In terms of the lifestyle typology, for example, preretirement males who are obsessively instrumental, may prove to be those who at time two, after retirement, embark on a round of exhausting, frenzied activities which overtax their physical resources.

CONCLUSION

This model focuses on change in the relationship between global values and concrete goals, and on change in the articulation between the values/goals constellation and behavior in adulthood. It further provides for relating these changes to certain dimensions of self-perception and of social norm and social network perception. The model thus has promise as a limited but practicable paradigm for making preliminary assessments of the comparative importance of intrinsic factors vs. socialization processes associated with trends toward growth, stabilization, or regression in adult life.

REFERENCES

Allport, G. W. *Pattern and growth in personality.* New York: Holt, Rinehart & Winston, [1937], 1961.

Berger, P. *Invitation to sociology: A humanistic perspective.* New York: Doubleday, Anchor, 1963.

Berger, P. & Luckmann, T. *The social construction of reality.* New York: Doubleday, 1966.

Birren, J. E. (Ed.) *Relations of development and aging.* Springfield, Ill.: Charles C Thomas, 1964.

Boulding, K. E. *The image.* Ann Arbor: The University of Michigan Press, [1956], 1966.

Brim, O. G., Jr. Adult socialization. In J. A. Clausen (Ed.) *Socialization and society.* Boston: Little, Brown, 1968.

Bühler, C., & Massarik, F. (Eds.) *The course of human life.* New York: Springer Publishing Company, 1968.

Butler, R. N. The life review: An interpretation of reminiscence in the aged. *Psychiatry,* 1963, *26* (1), 65-76.

Caro, F. G. Social class and attitudes of youth relevant for the realization of adult goals. *Social Forces*, 1966, *44*, 492–498.

Chinoy, E. *Automobile workers and the American dream*. Garden City, New York: Doubleday, 1955.

Clark, M. & Anderson, B. G. *Culture and aging: An anthropological study of older Americans*. Springfield, Ill.: Charles C Thomas, 1967.

Clausen, J. A. Personality measurement in the Oakland growth study. In. J. Birren (Ed.) *Relations of development and aging*. Springfield, Ill.: Charles C Thomas, 1964.

– – – A historical and comparative view of socialization theory and research. In J. A. Clausen (Ed.) *Socialization and Society*. Boston: Little, Brown, 1968.

– – – The life course of individuals. In M. W. Riley, M. Johnson., & A. Fonner (Eds.) *Essays in the sociology of age stratification*. New York: Russell Sage Foundation, in press.

Cumming, E. New thoughts on the theory of disengagement. In R. Kastenbaum (Ed.) *New thoughts on old age*. New York: Springer Publishing Company, 1968.

Cumming, E. & Henry, W. E. *Growing old: The process of disengagement*. New York: Basic Books, 1961.

Erickson, E. H. *Childhood and society*. New York: W. W. Norton & Co., 1950.

––– Identity and the life cycle. *Psychological Issues*, 1959. 1 (1, 1).

– – – *Gandhi's truth*. New York: W. W. Norton & Co., 1969.

Gutmann, D. L. The country of old men. *Occasional papers in Gerontology, No. 5*. Ann Arbor: University of Michigan Press, 1969.

Havighurst, R. J. The nature and values of meaningful free-time activity. In R. W. Kleemeier (Ed.) *Aging and leisure*. New York: Oxford University Press, 1961 a.

– – – Successful aging. *Gerontologist*, 1961 b, *1*, 8-13.

Havighurst, R. J., Neugarten, B. L. & Tobin, S. S. Disengagement, personality, and life satisfaction in the later years. In P. F. Hansen (Ed.) *Age with a future: Proceedings of the Sixth International Congress of Gerontology, Copenhagen*. Copenhagen: Munksgaard, 1964.

Henry, W. E. The theory of intrinsic disengagement. In P. F. Hansen (ed.) *Age with a future: Proceedings of the Sixth International Congress of Gerontology, Copenhagen*. Copenhagen: Munksgaard, 1964.

– – – Engagement and disengagement: Toward a theory of adult development. In R. Kastenbaum (Ed.) *Contributions to the psychobiology of aging*. New York: Springer Publishing Company, 1965.

Hyman, H. Reflections on reference groups. *Public Opinion Quarterly*, 1960, *24*, 383-396.

Inkeles, A. Society, social structure and child socialization. In J. A. Clausen (Ed.) *Socialization and society*. Boston: Little, Brown, 1968.

Kilby, R. W. Personal goals of Indian and American university students. *Journal of Humanistic Psychology*, 1965, *5*, 122-146.

Kornhauser, A. *Mental health of the industrial worker: A Detroit study*. New York: John Wiley & Sons, 1965.

Kuhlen, R. G. Changing personal adjustment during the adult years. In J. E. Anderson (Ed.) *Psychological aspects of aging*. Washington, D.C.: American Psychological Association, 1956.

– – – Developmental changes in motivation during the adult years. In J. Birren (Ed.) *Relations of development and aging*. Springfield, Ill.: Charles C Thomas, 1964.

Lowenthal, M. F. Some potentialities of a life cycle approach to the study of retirement. In F. Carp (Ed.) *Retirement*. New York: Behavioral Publications, in press.

Lowenthal, M. F., Berkman, P. L. & Associates, *Aging and mental disorder in San Francisco: A social psychiatric study*. San Francisco: Jossey-Bass, Inc., 1967.

Lowenthal, M. F. & Haven, C. Interaction and adaptation: Intimacy as a critical variable. *American Sociological Review*, 1968, *33*, 20-30.

Lowenthal, M. F., Spence, D. L. & Thurnher, M. Interplay of personal and social factors at transitional stages, In I. Rosow, Socialization to old age. NICHD, in press.

Maddox, G. L. Themes and issues in sociological theories of human aging. *Human Development*, 1970, *13*(1), 17-27.

Merton, R. K. *Social theory and social structure*. Glencoe, Ill.: The Free Press, 1957.

Murray, H. A. Toward a classification of interactions. In T. Parsons & E. Shils (Eds.) *Towards a general theory of action*. Cambridge, Mass.: Harvard University Press, 1962.

Neugarten, B. L. A developmental view of adult personality. In J. Birren (Ed.) *Relations of development and aging*. Springfield, Ill.: Charles C Thomas, 1964.

– – – Continuities and discontinuities of psychological issues in adult life. *Human Development*, 1969, *12*, 121-130.

– – – Adult personality: A developmental view. *Human Development*, 1966, 9(2), 61-73.

– – – Adaptation and the life cycle. *Journal of Geriatric Psychiatry*, in press.

Neugarten, B. L. & Associates. *Personality in middle and late life*. New York: Atherton Press, 1964.

Parsons, T. *The structure of social action*. New York: The Free Press of Glencoe, 1949.

Parsons, T. Boundary relations between sociocultural and personality systems. In R. Grinker (Ed.) *Toward a unified theory of human behavior*. New York: Basic Books, 1956.

––– *The social system*. New York: The Free Press of Glencoe, [1951], 1963.

Peter, L. J. & Hull, R. *The Peter principle*. New York: Bantam Books, 1969.

Pressey, S. L. & Kuhlen, R. G. *Psychological development through the life span*. New York: Harper and Row, 1957.

Reichard, S. F. L., Livson, F., & Petersen, P. G. *Aging and personality: A study of eighty-seven older men*. New York: John Wiley & Sons, 1962.

Riegel, K. F. History as a nomothetic science: Some generalizations from theory and research in developmental psychology. *The Journal of Social Issues*, 1969, *4*, 99-127.

Rosenberg, M. *Occupations and values*. Glencoe, Ill.: The Free Press, 1957.

Rosow, I. Forms and functions of adult socialization. *Social Forces*, 1965, *44*, 35-45.

Schaie, K. W. A general model for the study of developmental problems. *Psychological Bulletin*, 1965, *64*, 92-107.

––– Age changes and age differences. *The Gerontologist*, 1967, *7*(2-1), 128-133.

Smith, M. B. *Social psychology and human values*. Chicago: Aldine Publishing Company, 1969.

Thomae, H. Theory of aging and cognitive theory of personality. *Human Development*, 1970, *13*(1), 1-16.

White, R. W. Competence and the psychosexual stages of development. In M. R. Jones (Ed.) *Nebraska symposium on motivation*. Lincoln, Nebraska: University of Nebraska Press, 1960.

––– Motivation reconsidered: the concept of competence. In D. W. Fiske & S. R. Maddi (Eds.) *Functions of varied experience*. Homewood, Ill.: Dorsey Press, 1961.

Williams, R. H. & Wirths, C. G. *Lives through the years*. New York: Atherton Press, 1965.

chapter 2

NO EXIT: A SYMBOLIC INTERACTIONIST PERSPECTIVE ON AGING*

Victor W. Marshall, Ph.D.

Social gerontological studies and, in particular, studies of socialization for old age, reflect a normative bias, almost completely ignoring a dynamic or processual view of human nature and society. The symbolic interactionist approach posits a general, or orienting perspective as an alternative to the normative approach. Within the perspective, the concepts of "status passage" and "career" show promise of directing useful research concerning the ways in which individuals are able to fashion their lives during the later years. In this paper I characterize the contrast between a *normative* and a *symbolic-interactionist* approach to aging, demonstrate the normative bias in current approaches to socialization manifested in the gerontological literature, and indicate some ways in which the career and status passage concepts are particularly fruitful.

THE NORMATIVE BIAS OF SOCIALIZATION THEORY

Most sociology, including that utilized in gerontology, reflects a normative bias. This point is made by Allan Dawe, whose distinction between "the two sociologies" I employ [1]. Dawe sees the predominant theoretical tradition of sociology as stemming from a conservative reaction to the French revolution. This sociology stresses the problem of order, the question of why there is not a "war of each against all." The solution to the Hobbesian problem places the link between the individual and society as near-perfect. Through socialization processes conceived as highly efficient, the individual internalizes roles. Roles, the expectations for behavior or complexes of norms appropriate for the

* This is a greatly revised version of a paper presented at a symposium, "Symbolic-Interaction Approaches to Theory and Research in Adulthood," 28th Annual Meeting, Gerontological Society, Louisville, Kentucky, October 1975.

incumbent of a given status or position, provide the mediating links between the individual and the society; for society is made up of role-behavior. Internalization of roles thus implies that social norms became *constitutive*, rather than merely regulative, of the self. Conformity, then, is seen as normal, and not needing explanation. Only deviance needs to be explained, and the explanation rests on a notion of incomplete or warped socialization. A major contemporary exponent of this view is, of course, Talcott Parsons. Essentially the same description of normative sociology is given in Wrong's paper, "The Oversocialized Conception of Man in Modern Sociology" [2], in which he notes the Durkheimian influence, and goes on to say, "Parsons developed this view that social norms are constitutive rather than merely regulative of human nature before he was influenced by psycho-analytic theory, but Freud's theory of the superego has become the source and model for the conception of the internalization of social norms that today plays so important a part in sociological thinking." When Matilda Riley and Associates [3, pp. 952-953] draw their approach to socialization in old age, "mainly from the work of Parsons . . ." they adopt this sociology of order conception. Other major exponents are Neugarten [4, 5] and Rosow [6].

Though taking issue with Neugarten and Riley on a number of points, Irving Rosow [6], whose recent monograph has done us all a great service in summarizing much data concerning later life socialization, does not differ in overall perspective. His approach is also a sociology of order conception of socialization:

> Adult socialization is the process of inculcating new values and behavior appropriate to adult positions and group memberships. These changes are normally internalized in the course of induction or training procedures, whether formal or informal. They result in new images, expectations, skills, and norms as the person defines himself and as others view him [6, p. 3].

Note the normative assumptions. He continues [6, p. 32]: "Successful socialization produces conformity to *shared* expectations about values and behavior." Socialization is not always perfect, however, and indeed this is a cornerstone of Rosow's argument. "The process does not function like a social die which stamps out uniform social products. Socialization results do vary . . ." However, variance from perfect socialization is not "normal," for, as this sentence continues, " . . . deviance may result from many causes." Rosow argues that "the transition to old age in America represents a special problem in adult socialization . . ." [6, p. 117], because this transition differs from "normal status passages" in marking a movement

> . . . (1) to a *devalued position* (2) with *ambiguous norms,* (3) *role discontinuity,* and (4) *status loss* (5) that mobilizes *low motivation* or resistance to possible socialization (6) whose processes would be set in *informal contexts.* Thereby, on each factor, aging reverses the optimal conditions of socialization . . . [6, pp. 117-118].

According to Rosow there cannot be adequate socialization for old age because clear expectations for conduct in old age do not exist, and because aging individuals have neither the opportunity nor the incentive to internalize those expectations that do exist. This may well be the case, but it might also be that these considerations represent a rather restricted issue; for it is only within a normative sociology that internalization of *shared* expectations is seen as important.

A NON-NORMATIVE APPROACH TO SOCIALIZATION

The second, less dominant sociological tradition outlined by Dawe encompasses the symbolic interactionist approach to sociology.[1] This tradition, rooted in the Enlightenment impulse toward liberation, focuses on the ways in which individuals seek to gain control or mastery over their situations, relationships, and institutions. As with the *philosophes,* the concern is with ". . . how humans could regain *control* over essentially man-made institutions and historical situations." The degree of sharedness of norms is not pre-judged: "There is no postulate of consensus or, for that matter, of cooperation, conflict or constraint." [1]   Rather than seeing order as obtaining in society because of semi-perfect internalization of the society by individuals, through socialization, this second sociology sees any departure from a Hobbesian state of chaos or anarchy in terms of two concepts: a concept of *central meaning,* and a concept of *control.*

First, central meanings held by the individual (as contrasted to values shared by the members of a collectivity) are employed by him to link his biography together. Identity thus becomes an important concept. Let us call identity "a sense of sameness or continuity of the organization of selves over time." This definition is congruent with the usages of Erikson [7]. The meaning attributed by an individual to his biography may be termed his individual or *felt* identity; that view of himself (his selves) displayed for others may be termed his personal or *presented* identity: the meanings which others attribute to his self (or selves) may be termed his *social* identity. These distinctions are drawn from Goffman [8]. The "action" is in the attempts by individuals to negotiate, in terms of felt identity, in a world where others cast social identities on them. One strategy actors use is through presentation of self (presented identity). The dimension of action is intrinsically related to meaning, for the self arises in social interaction, and situations which bring selves together are controlled by the imposition of meaning.

Second, "to control a situation is to impose one's definition upon the other actors in that situation. The concept of control refers essentially to social relationships

---

[1] Dawe calls the "first" sociology a "sociology of order," and the "second" a "sociology of control." I will use the terms "normative" and "non-normative" respectively. The latter encompasses *selected* strands of symbolic interactionism, phenomenology, neo-Marxist, and ethnomethodological sociologies.

whose properties cannot be reduced to the individual definitions and courses of action from which they emerge." [1] *Individuals negotiate with one another to work out some sense and semblance of order* [9, 10] , and that sense of order is always changing and subject to re-negotiation, as individuals bring together their biographically-meaningful lines of action and attempt to exercise some control or power [9, 10]. Norms are not something "out there" to be learned, and internalized, and which thence determine behavior; rather, norms are viewed as claims involved in, and outcomes of, continuous negotiation processes. As Blumer tells us, this is so not only for novel forms of interaction, but for habitual or repetitive interaction [11, pp. 18-19] :

> . . . we have to recognize that even in the case of pre-established and repetitive joint action each instance of such joint action has to be formed anew . . . . Repetitive and stable joint action is just as much a result of an interpretative process as is a new form of joint action that is being developed for the first time . . . . A gratuitous acceptance of the concepts of norms, values, social rules, and the like should not blind the social scientist to the fact that any one of them is subtended by a process of social interaction . . . . *It is the social process in group life that creates and upholds the rules, not the rules that create and uphold group life.* (stress mine)

Norms are *invoked* in social interaction. We utilize conceptions of appropriate behavior in our attempts to negotiate with others. We *sometimes* do as others say. But our conformity to the expectations of others (and their conformity to ours) is less massive than the normative, or social order, perspective would suggest. Our life with others is not so automatic or rule-following as, for example, Neugraten suggests [12] :

> . . . every society has a system of social expectations regarding age-appropriate behavior. The individual passes through a socially-regulated cycle from birth to death . . . a succession of socially-delineated age-statuses, each with its recognized rights, duties, and obligations . . . . This normative pattern is adhered to, more or less consistently, by most persons . . . .

Neugarten, like Rosow, is an exemplary scholar of this general persuasion. The disagreement between Rosow and Neugarten concerning the existence of norms for the aged should not mask their fundamental agreement. Rosow argues that normative expectations for the aged are not clear, and he bemoans this fact [6, pp. 10-11, 52, 54-79]. Neugarten argues that behavior in the aged is under the strong influence of norms [4, 5, 12] :

> . . . For any social group it can be demonstrated that norms and age expectations act as a system of social controls, as prods and brakes upon behavior, in some instances hastening an event, in others, delaying it [12].

For Neugarten, normatively-regulated old age exists as the general pattern and is *normal;* for Rosow it does not exist, but is nonetheless viewed as *normal.*

Turning to the related concept of role, it is noteworthy that Neugarten turns not to Mead, but to Parsons and Shils for her conception of *role* as "a sector of an individual actor's range of action . . . also a specific set of behaviors having a particular function for a social institution . . . ." People are socialized to perform roles, and "the life cycle can be seen as a succession of roles and changing role constellations, and a certain order and predictability of behavior occurs over time as individuals move through a succession of roles." [4]

This position stands in marked contrast to that of the symbolic interactionists, who reject a notion of role as equivalent to a die-press which stamps out behavior. As Turner suggests [13]:

> The actor is not the occupant of a position for which there is a neat set of rules — a culture or set of norms — but a person who must act in the perspective supplied in part by his relationship to others whose actions reflect roles that he must identify . . . testing inferences about the role of alter is a continuing element in interaction. Hence the tentative character of the individual's own role definition and performance is never wholly suspended.

The human capacity for socially *constructing* reality is emphasized by the symbolic interactionist, in marked contrast to the normative sociology's emphasis on the human capacity for incorporating and internalizing an external reality. The imagery of the actor portrays an individual who searches for meaning, who constructs his identity, and who seeks to direct his interactions with others in ways compatible with his sense of identity. As Dawe argues, the key notion of this "second sociology"

> . . . is that of autonomous man, able to realize his full potential and to create a truly human social order only when freed from external restraint. Society is thus the creation of its members; the product of their construction of meaning, and of the action and relationships through which they attempt to impose that meaning on their historical situations.

From the sociology of social control perspective, the concept of socialization comes to be viewed as a *gloss,* a short-hand common-sensical way of describing the ways in which people interact with one another over the course of the life cycle, and come to attribute meaning to their interaction [14]. It is a shorthand way of talking about the ways people *realize* their world in the dual sense of that term: "come to know," and "bring to reality." [15, 16, pp. 1-2]

Those sociologists of aging who find themselves in sympathy with the premises of this "second sociology" will risk seduction if they uncritically continue to employ the concept "socialization," for that concept implies socialization to something, and that something is a shared set of values and ideas. Those who believe that human beings are characterized by a considerable amount of intentionality or voluntarism, and that there is not a great deal of concensus governing human conduct at *any* stage of the life cycle (let alone old age), may find it profitable to theorize in terms of the vocabulary of symbolic interactionism. At the very least, gerontologists would do well to empirically assess the extent to which either of these general theoretical perspectives facilitates an understanding of the processes of aging. In the remainder of the paper I restrict my objectives to some suggestions of research lines, illustrated by a consideration of one particular aspect of aging. This represents my continuing efforts to develop a more satisfactory interpretation of data already discussed [17–20].

AGING AS A CAREER OR STATUS PASSAGE

As Dawe notes, the capacity of an individual to control the situations of his life is differentially distributed [1]:

> It depends partly on the nature and scope of situational definitions; partly on the relationship, in terms of projected outcomes, between the consequent courses of action; and partially on differential access to facilities and subjection to limiting conditions . . . the extent to which control depends upon normative, calculative and/or coercive mechanisms become empirical questions.

The notions of career and status passage are useful in directing us to some appropriate empirical questions. To speak of aging as a status passage is to point to a person negotiating a passage from one age-linked status to another, and then to others, finally coming to the end of the passage through life, at death. The older notion of "career" is closely related to that of "status passage." Both concepts correspond in the temporal domain to the negotiated order concept discussed above:

> Just as an orientation toward the solution of everyday problems and the ongoing negotiation of social order link people and their activities in a "horizontal" way, the activities of individuals themselves are linked "vertically" over time. The concept of "career" captures the nature of this vertical linkage [21, p. 177].

A career or a status passage may be thought of either from the perspective of the individual or from an objective perspective. Everett Hughes, who developed the present meaning of the career concept, makes the distinction [22, p. 137].

> However one's ambitions and accomplishments turn, they involve some sequence of relations to organized life. In a highly and rigidly structured society, a career consists, *objectively*, of a series of status (sic) and clearly defined offices. In a freer one, the individual has more latitude for creating his own position or choosing from a number of existing ones . . . but unless complete disorder reigns, there will be typical sequences of position, achievement, responsibility, and even of adventure. The social order will set limits upon the individual's orientation of his life, both as to direction of effort and as to interpretation of its meaning. *Subjectively,* a career is the moving perspective in which the person sees his life as whole and interprets the meaning of his various attributes, actions, and the things which happen to him. (stress added)

A number of dimensions of status passages, or careers, are outlined in the works of Becker, Glaser and Strauss, and Hughes.[2] *Objectively,* any status passage can be defined in terms of physical and social time and space. The duration may be long or short, and given meaning as such by others. The passage may be treated as preparatory, initiatory, educative, selective, or ritualistic. The passage may involve physical movement, or horizontal or lateral movement in social status. It may be viewed by others as desirable or undesirable, inevitable or optional, voluntary or involuntary, reversible or irreversible, repeatable or unique. The passage may occur collectively, aggregatively, or solo. It may be guided or controlled by others, or self, or collectively guided or controlled. If undergone with others, the degree to which co-passagees may communicate with others at the same stage in the passage, or ahead of them, might vary. The passage may vary in moral authority or societal legitimation.

Subjectively, people may be aware, in different degree, that they are actually undergoing a passage. Awareness of any of the aforementioned objective properties of the passage may vary. One may or may not decide, for example, to voluntarily accept an inevitable passage (e.g., to accept one's dying). One may attempt to seize, or may surrender, control over the passage. The passage, or subpassages may be viewed as of crucial or trivial importance.

This listing of objective and subjective properties of status passages (or careers) is not exhaustive. What does this list have to do with socialization theory? Socialization theory in the normative tradition postulates that the lives of aging individuals will be shaped by the extent to which shared norms exist to define acceptable behavior, and the extent to which these norms are internalized. Status passage theory postulates that the lives of aging individuals will be shaped by themselves, in the context of others, as they manipulate these properties and properties like them. Viewing later life as a status passage or career removes the artificial boundary which normative theorists have established between the individual and society. "Socialization," in the normative tradition, is a concept which provides an important link between the abstraction "individual" and the abstractions "society" or "group"; but these abstractions, I argue, mislead us. If life is viewed as a sequence of meaningful negotiations with others, we do not need the abstract concept "society," and hence no longer need the concept "socialization" *as an abstract concept,* except when discussing its use in previous work. There remains, however, one useful way to employ the term "socialization." The term may be used to refer to concrete attempts by some agents to shape the careers or status passages of others.

The symbolic interactionist perspective is only one version (actually a collection of related versions) of a non-normative sociology [26]. Its emphasis on negotiation offers a vivid contrast to conventional socialization theory.

---

[2] The careers/status passage notion is central to much of Hughes' work [see 22, 25], and influenced Becker and Strauss during their time at the University of Chicago [23]. The properties of status passage outlined below draw on Becker, Hughes, and particularly Glaser and Strauss [24].

Within the symbolic interactionist approach the "careers" or "status passage" concept represents, in turn, only one strand of theory which emphasizes meaningful passage of an individual over time.

I will now suggest the fruitfulness of this approach to understanding later life. The degree of control over the passage becomes of central importance for aging persons.

NO EXIT: AGING AS A TERMINAL STATUS PASSAGE

By calling this paper "No Exit," I do not wish to imply that there is no exit *from* the aging status passage; only that there is no exit *during* the passage. People can exit from the marital status passage at virtually any time (through desertion, separation or divorce); they can skip school, have an abortion, quit their jobs. But aging, as noted by Glaser and Strauss, and as is evident to us all, is an *inevitable* status passage [24, p. 15]. There is an exit at the end, in death, but there is no way to escape having to go through the passage. This fact, as writers such as Heidegger have told us so well, places a special accent on the passage. Aging is a status passage unlike any other.

This point may become clearer by turning to research on medical students. Some studies, notably *The Student Physician*, stress the future-orientation of the students [27]. As they pass through the status-passage of the school, the students think of themselves as nascent professionals. The *Boys in White*, study found the students preoccupied with their present status [28]. They were too busy learning to be students to be concerned with learning to be doctors. They focused, not on the outcome of the passage, but on the passage itself. Their concerns, so evident in the *Boys in White* monograph, were to gain as much *control* over their status passage as possible.

The theoretical point I wish to stress is that individuals may be preoccupied in different measure either with "getting out" of the passage or with the passage itself. Think of a brief, and highly ritualized status passage, the marriage ceremony. The concerns of the participants here are mixed. There is great concern that the passage itself go off appropriately. That concern is perhaps felt most acutely by others who are managing the ritual, such as the parents. The passagees themselves, in most cases, presumably are oriented primarily to their shared future.

Although control over the passage is but one of many dimensions of status passage, it is particularly important in the case of aging, for there is no exit from the passage (except through death). The passage itself is all there is. With aging comes recognition that time is running out [16]. Life, which has so often been viewed as a preparation for *something to come,* becomes preparation for dying and for death itself. No future lies beyond the passage, only the passage and its termination become relevant. Elsewhere I have argued that preparation for death involves the endeavor to make sense of death itself and to make sense of one's biography. This theme appears in disengagement theory, developmental

ego-psychology, and in Butler's conception of the life review process [17, 19].
The status passage of aging becomes expanded backward to encompass the
entire biography of the person. Neugarten makes a similar argument in
developmental terms [12, 29].

We human beings are fundamentally motivated to endow our experience in
this world with meaning. Control over our biographies is sought through the
creative re-construction of the past through reminiscence. I have argued
elsewhere that this process is most successful when it is conducted socially [17].

Glaser and Strauss [24, p. 15] argue that inevitable or non-reversible status
passages require "that there be institutions and organizations to manage, direct
and control them."[3] But, as Rosow has shown, there is little institutional or
organizational control over the inevitable and irreversible status passage of aging.
Sub-passages which intersect in later life do, of course, come under institutional
and organizational control: illness and chronicity as well as death and dying
come under the control of the health care institution. Poverty, which is often
age-related, brings the passage under organizational control within the social
service/welfare institution. But significant areas of aging peoples' lives come
under no-one's control. This point is made most strongly by Rosow. While
Rosow sees this as a "failure of socialization," we see it rather differently when
we look at it from the symbolic interactionist perspective.

Absence of "socializing agents" may be cause for alarm or rejoicing, as is
evident if we contrast the perspectives held by an adolescent and by his parents
concerning the chaperoning of a party. When adults are not around to chaperone
adolescents, their activity does not break down into a "war of each against all."
Rather, they mutually regulate their behavior, negotiating among themselves for
some measure of individual and collective control over their situations (which, in
this instance, frequently involves much competition if not conflict). Perhaps as
adults enter the status passage of late life, something similar happens when they
find themselves without chaperones, or "socializing agents." Perhaps they are
able to work things out for themselves.

Institutionalization severely threatens the aged's ability to maintain status
passage control, for so much is structured for them, and compliance with
institutional routines is deemed necessary to keep things "running smoothly."
(See [18, 20, 30–32] for descriptions of a range of institutionalization.
Theoretical dimensions appear in [33] and [34].) Only contrast the typical
resident of a nursing home with the "bag lady" described by Sharon Curtin [35,
Ch. 6]: "Tough, mean, ignorant. Formed by her society. But she was still
quite a lady, quite a woman. She survived. She managed." [35, p. 91] The
"bag lady" described by Curtin managed to maintain high degrees of status
passage control by cultivating great skills in managing the urban environment,

---

[3] "Chronic disease, dying and the life cycle (aging) are the inevitable passages that easily
come to mind. It is difficult to think of others which cannot be reversed or blocked
somehow, by someone, no matter how inevitable they appear." [24, p. 15]

and also by frightening other people away from her by real or presented craziness. Isolation was the price she paid for control.

It might, in fact, be argued, and is at any rate worth exploring, that status passage control becomes a dilemma for the aging whenever they encounter persons who wish to shape their passages [5, pp. 84-85]. This is patently clear in cases where the others employ criteria for desired behavior which contradict the desires of the aging person to maintain personal control. Examples would include the subjection of the older person to a hospital, or nursing home routine [31—36]. These cases customarily are marked by bargaining over timing.

Older people may be fortunate that, as Rosow shows, there are few norms to guide their behavior in later life, and few socializing agents or agencies [6]. This situation leaves the aging at least relatively free from normative constraints (if often not free from objective constraints such as poverty, isolation, declining health). It is hoped that in this relative freedom they can seek, with others, to construct a passage through their last years which maximizes personal control.

It is a fundamental postulate of a symbolic-interactionist social psychology that reality is socially constructed and sustained. This implies that *any and all aspects of status passage control can be viewed as socially constructed.* Hochschild [37] gives us a portrayal of a group of older people who are given the opportunity to construct a way of life which gives them relatively high equanimity in the last years (as have I, [18, 20]). She also points out [37, p. 139] that Merril Court, the apartment building community she studied, "was an unexpected community, an exception." Hochschild may be viewed as utilizing a sociology of social control perspective. She emphasizes that people gain some measure of control over their lives *interactionally.* Community facilitates the gaining of status passage control, whereas isolation prevents it [37, p. 139]:

> Not all who are isolated feel lonely and not all who feel lonely are isolated. But even for the confirmed urban hermit, isolation may be involuntary. Or rather, the choices of whom to see and talk with are made within an increasingly narrow band of alternatives.

The objective and subjective aspects of career or status passage must thus be brought together in any analysis. A study focused at the level of the individual's subjective status passage must of necessity shed light on objective properties of the passage. As Hughes puts it, " . . . a study of careers . . . may be expected to reveal the nature and 'working constitution' of a society . . . . In the course of a career the person finds his place within these forms, carries on his active life with reference to other people, and interprets the meaning of the one life he has to live." [25] The degree of freedom to manipulate objective conditions (physical or social) is undoubtedly less than the degree of freedom to give a subjectively acceptable accent to these conditions. None of these illustrations make reference to the internalization of shared norms concerning appropriate age-related behavior; yet they all refer to older people making their way through the later years.

CONCLUSION

I have suggested that socialization theory in gerontology (including the work of such exemplars as Neugarten, Riley, and Rosow) has focused on issues stemming from a normative perspective in which socialization is viewed as a process through which individuals come to internalize expectations for age-related conduct. While not denying the utility of this approach, I have argued that at the very least it ignores many important aspects of aging; and that its emphasis on shared expectations, and the failure to provide adequate socialization (in terms of the perspective) for old age, presents a distorted image of the processes of aging. Drawing on a distinct tradition in sociology which emphasizes the human capacity to construct and share meanings, and the human tendency to attempt to control, through symbolic interaction, situations in keeping with biographically meaningful intentions, I suggested the utility of the "status passage" and "career" concepts. These concepts, which have considerable currency within the symbolic-interactionist tradition, lead to an enumeration of various properties of objective and subjective careers. The status passage of aging was described as a distinct career because there is "no exit" from it. Aging is one of the very few inevitable and irreversible status passages; and it of course encompasses sub-passages such as childhood and dying which are also inevitable and irreversible. But aging in later life is additionally distinctive in that the passage leads nowhere but to death. Because it is not preparatory for other statuses, as are many other status passages, passagees come to focus on issues of controlling the passage. Issues of status passage control were illustrated in terms of the subjective-objective distinction. Subjective status passage control centers on the construction and maintenance of identity in later life, and the relationship of identity to preparation for death. As I have explored these issues elsewhere, they were only touched on here. Status passage control was then explored in relation to the situation of the aged in relation to others. One set of others might be deemed "agents of socialization," and includes those who socialize the aged into homes for the aged and hospitals. These reduce the amount of individual control which people may exert, whether they traverse the passage solo or in aggregate or collective fashion. Others can, however, assist in maintaining or creating status passage control, for reality is constructed *socially*. The isolation of many aged constitutes an objective fact which forces them, in a sense, to live in a reality constructed by others, rather than controlling their passages through old age in a community of others.

One final point must be made. The status passage conception of later life is important, I believe, chiefly because it recognizes the human capacity to endow experience with meaning. This recognition is viewed by many social scientists as either an untested assumption or a scientifically unfruitful one. To me it is manifestly clear that our world is a world of meanings. Moreover, the related assumption that people do not always agree on the meanings follows logically from this very dispute. Divergences in meanings point to the importance of active interpretation processes, and in turn suggest the importance of the "control" or "power" aspects of this perspective. That older people do not possess complete freedom to construct a world of their choice is patently manifest. To say that our world is a world of meanings is not to say it is a world of ideas alone. The symbolic interactionist perspective, with its emphasis on the *processes* of negotiation, emphasizes this. The perspective has much to offer gerontology.

ACKNOWLEDGEMENTS

I am grateful to Jon Hendricks, Donald F. Spence, and particularly D. Ralph Matthews for critical comments on this paper.

REFERENCES

1. A. Dawe, The Two Sociologies, *British Journal of Sociology, 21,* pp. 207-218, 1970.
2. D. Wrong, The Oversocialized Conception of Man in Modern Sociology, *American Sociological Review, 26,* pp. 183-193, April 1961.
3. M. W. Riley, A. Foner, B. Hess, and M. Toby, Socialization for the Middle and Later Years, In: D. R. Goslin (ed.), *Handbook of Socialization Theory and Research,* Rand McNally, Chicago, 1969.
4. B. Neugarten and N. Datan, Sociological Perspectives on the Life Cycle, In: P. Baltes and K. W. Schaie (eds.), *Life-Span Developmental Psychology: Personality and Socialization,* Academic Press, New York, 1973.
5. B. Neugarten, J. Moore, and J. Lowe, Age Norms, Age Constraints, and Adult Socialization, *American Journal of Sociology, 70:6,* pp. 710-717, 1965.
6. I. Rosow, *Socialization to Old Age,* University of California Press, Berkeley, 1974.
7. E. Erikson, Identity and the Life Cycle, *Psychological Issues, No. 1,* 1959.
8. E. Goffman, *Stigma,* Prentice-Hall, Englewood Cliffs, 1963.
9. A. Strauss, L. Schatzman, D. Ehrlich, R. Bucher, and M. Sabshin, The Hospital and Its Negotiated Order, In: E. Freidson (ed.), *The Hospital in Modern Society,* Collier-Macmillan, London, 1963.
10. E. Goffman, *The Presentation of Self in Everyday Life,* Doubleday Anchor, Garden City, 1969.
11. H. Blumer, *Symbolic Interactionism,* Prentice Hall, Englewood Cliffs, 1969.
12. B. Neugarten, Dynamics of Transition of Middle Age to Old Age, *Journal of Geriatric Psychiatry, 4:1,* pp. 71-87, Fall 1970.
13. R. Turner, Role-Taking: Process versus Conformity, In: A. Rose (ed.), *Human Nature and Social Processes,* Houghton-Mifflin, Boston, 1962.
14. R. MacKay, Conceptions of Children and Models of Socialization, In: H. P. Dreitzel (ed.), *Recent Sociology No. 5,* Macmillan, New York, 1973.
15. D. Rafky, Phenomenology and Socialization: Some Comments on the Assumptions Underlying Socialization Theory, *Sociological Analysis, 32:1,* 1971.
16. A. Weisman, *The Realization of Death,* Jason Aronson, New York, 1974.

17. V. W. Marshall, The Life Review as a Social Process, Paper presented at 27th Annual Scientific Meeting of Gerontological Society, Portland, Oregon, 1974.
18. V. W. Marshall, Socialization for Impending Death in a Retirement Village, *American Journal of Sociology, 80:*5, pp. 1224-1244, 1975.
19. V. W. Marshall, Age and Awareness of Finitude in Developmental Gerontology, *Omega, 6:*2, pp. 113-129, 1975.
20. V. W. Marshall, Organizational Features of Terminal Status Passage in Residential Facilities for the Aged, *Urban Life: A Journal of Analytic Ethnography, 4:*3, pp. 349-368, 1975.
21. J. Hewitt, *Self and Society,* Allyn and Bacon, Boston, 1976.
22. E. C. Hughes, Cycles, Turning Points, and Careers, Reprinted in E. C. Hughes *The Sociological Eye: Selected Papers on Institutions and Race,* The University of Chicago Press, Chicago, 1971.
23. H. S. Becker and A. Strauss, Careers, Personality and Adult Socialization, *American Journal of Sociology, 62,* pp. 253-263, November 1956.
24. B. Glaser and A. Strauss, *Status Passage,* Aldine, Atherton, Chicago, 1971.
25. E. C. Hughes, Institutional Office and the Person, *American Journal of Sociology, 43,* pp. 404-413, November 1937.
26. B. Meltzer, J. Petras and L. Reynolds, *Symbolic Interactionism,* Routledge and Kegan Paul, London, 1975.
27. R. K. Merton, G. Reader, and P. Kendall (eds.), *The Student Physician,* Harvard University Press, Cambridge, 1957.
28. H. S. Becker, B. Geer, E. C. Hughes, and A. Strauss, *Boys in White,* The University of Chicago Press, Chicago, 1956.
29. B. Neugarten, Adult Personality: A Developmental View, *Human Development, 9,* pp. 61-73, 1966.
30. K. Calkins, Time: Perspectives, Markings, and Styles of Usage, *Social Problems, 17,* pp. 487-501, Spring 1970.
31. E. Gustafson, Dying: The Career of the Nursing Home Patient, *Journal of Health and Social Behavior, 13,* pp. 226-235, September.
32. J. Posner, Notes on the Negative Implications of Being Competent in a Home for the Aged, *International Journal of Aging and Human Development, 5:*4, pp. 357-364, 1974.
33. R. Bennett and L. Nahemow, Institutional Totality and Criteria of Social Adjustment in Residences for the Aged, *Journal of Social Issues, 21:*4, pp. 44-75, 1965.
34. E. Goffman, *Asylums,* Doubleday Anchor, Garden City, 1961.
35. S. Curtin, *Nobody Ever Died of Old Age,* Little, Brown, Boston, 1972.
36. J. Roth, *Timetables,* Bobbs-Merril, Indianapolis, 1963.
37. A. Hochschild, *The Unexpected Community,* Prentice-Hall, Englewood Cliffs, 1973.

chapter 3

SOCIAL AND PSYCHOLOGICAL DETERMINANTS OF ADAPTATION*

Morton A. Lieberman, Ph.D.

Introduction

Although the concepts and methodology of social psychology are wide-ranging, a strict reading of gerontological research suggests that only a limited number of concepts have generated the vast majority of research efforts. Foremost, of course, is role theory; its influence has been manifest since the inception of organized efforts at research on aging. Of more indirect influence are the classical psychological dilemmas centering on personality conceptions—intrinsic personality characteristics in contrast to situational determinants. Much of what is currently portrayed as personality perspectives in aging reflects social psychological influences. Concern with transition events as major shaping influences, an emphasis on adaptation to crisis, the role of environmental contexts, whether they be kinship networks or total environments such as institutions, all reflect a particular emphasis of a field which has its theoretical, if not its methodological, roots in classical social psychological thought.

From this perspective, most social gerontologists are "hidden" social psychologists or at least fellow travelers. Obviously, however, such a generalization does little to grapple with the specific issues to which the symposium is addressed. Towards this goal, this paper will focus on adaptation, a topic within aging that is both important in its own right and one in which a reasonable amount of research exists. The frequent attention that adaptation has been given by investigators whose perspectives illustrate a range of frameworks, from a purely personologist through social psychological to sociological, makes it particularly relevant.

Research evidence generally suggests that: successful adaptation in old age is the rule rather than the exception; there seems to be no intrinsic connection

* This investigation was supported by Administration on Aging Grant No. 93-P-57425/5 from the Department of Health, Education, and Welfare, Office of Human Development, and by Research Scientist Award No. 1-KO5-MH-20342 from the National Institute of Mental Health.

between age and social integration; social integration generally is associated with well-being or mental health; and social class is generally associated with well-being or mental health.

These four empirical generalizations on adaptation provide considerable space for explanation and speculation. Personally, I find the empirical evidence that age bears little relationship to most measures of well-being or mental distress the most intriguing and perplexing, for the customary explanatory models based on stress or social context suggest that the findings would be quite the contrary.

Two social-psychological frameworks frequently used to account for failures or successes in adaptation emphasize environmental determinism based either on stress or on social context, usually defined as resources. Whether the concern is analyzing the relationship noted between social class and mental health, or between age and mental health, stress models emphasize differences among age or class groups with regard to the frequency, intensity, or type of social surroundings that induce stress within members of that group. Role theory is more frequently used to describe the environmentalist view in accounting for adaptive failures in later life. Role attrition is characteristic of the last stage of life, and this source of strain is used to explain the inverse relationship between well-being and age, an empirical relationship that by no means is consistent across studies.

Other investigators who are concerned with explaining the relationships between social class or age and mental health emphasize a social resource framework. Here the focus is on different characteristics of the person's social surroundings. Inquiries emphasize a diversity of parameters—role maintenance, functional social networks, macro-analysis of community characteristics, and micro-analysis of such variables as availability of significant others for intimacy. Fundamental to this approach is the notion that both low social class and advanced age are associated with characteristics of the person's social surround that are associated, in turn, with lowered well-being or increased mental disorder.

My intent is neither to present a completed empirical study nor a structured framework for understanding adaptation in the adult years. Rather, it is to raise questions, on the basis of some empirical observations, about the adequacy of current models.

The Study

These observations are from a study conducted at the University of Chicago by Bertram Cohler, Robert LeVine, Bernice Neugarten, and myself. We examined the interrelationships between culture and aging as factors influencing personality processes and adaptation in middle and late life. Variation across cultural groups was approximated by selecting respondents from three ethnic groups—Irish, Italian, and Polish Americans. The sample included 360 foreign-born men and women or their children, aged forty to eighty. Respondents were selected from census tracts in Chicago's standard metropolitan statistical area where the density of a particular ethnic group was greater than 8 per cent. Interviews canvassed target blocks pre-selected by the National Opinion Research Center. The complete interview, presented in survey research format, required about three and one-half hours to complete.

The information relevant to this paper arises from three major groups of indices: personality traits and processes, measures of adaptation, and characteristics of the person's social surround.

Indices

OF ADAPTATION

The study emphasized two of the numerous strategies for assessing level of adaptation. We assumed that a person's own view of his well-being could provide the most general measure and, therefore, chose the Life Satisfaction Index (LSI) as the most appropriate measure of this view because of its extensive use in the study of adult lives, its high stability, and its relatively "culture free" items. (In fact, we found mean scores in our population approximated scores reported by other investigators; furthermore, no differences in life satisfaction were found among the three ethnic groups studied.) Indices of breakdown underlay the other strategy. Several measures for indexing distress were employed—the Srole symptom check list (an indicator which has been shown to be affected by cultural differences), ratings of depression and anxiety based on samples of non-directed speech from our respondents (measures that may be less open to cultural influences), and a self-rating of health. Correlations between LSI and symptoms were $-.51$; between LSI and anxiety, $-.09$; between LSI and depression, $-.14$; and between LSI and health, $-.35$. The magnitude of the correlations, however, seriously underestimates the relationships. A division of the sample above or below the median for LSI and a categorization according to level of pathology (based on Langer's empirical criteria using symptoms) revealed that only 3 per cent of the sample defined as pathological have LSI's above the median.

OF PERSONALITY

1. Traits or dimensions (Dominance, Submission, Mastery Patterns, and Locus of Control) that have generally been shown to be relatively stable although showing developmental patterns over large spans of time.
2. Coping strategies.
3. How individuals organize and pattern their views of the world—Trust, Religious Attitudes, Authoritarianism, and Sources of Gratification.
4. Symbolic or inner life aspects that we felt were crucial for understanding adult development—Experienced Loss, Parental Images, and the Utilization of Reminiscence.

OF SOCIAL SURROUND

1. Structural relationship with regard to status—Social Class, Marital and Immigration Status, Social Mobility.
2. Relationship of the person to his or her social network—including perceived Amount and Type of Social Resource (e.g., friends and family) and Actual Social Context (e.g., the extensiveness of the family and friendship networks and number of relatives within walking distance), the degree to which the individual's activity pattern is related to the External World, the degree to which important Gratifications are arrived at via social contact, and the degree to which Intimacy with Spouse is an important source of gratification.
3. Characteristics of the person's neighborhood with regard to its Quality and the degree to which the person is Imbedded in a neighborhood area which contains large numbers of his or her ethnic group.

An Empirical Examination of Factors Influencing Level of Adaptation

Overall, the findings in this study about adaptation, whether assessed through indices of well-being or indices of pathology, match those reported in other studies on the relationship between structural characteristics and adaptation—no relationship between age and well-being, a modest relationship between social class and level of well-being, as well as rate of pathology, and no overwhelming evidence that social integration is functionally or intrinsically related to chronological age.

AFFECT OF THE ROLE OF LIFE STRESS

Examinations of differential adaptation frequently begin with the exploration of life events or the situational context which impinges upon the person and requires adaptational effort. Inherent in most theories of adaptation is a notion of stress—environmental demands placed on the organism requiring adaptive behavior.

We found in our study that the amount of stress, as measured by a Standard Life Event Index which assessed the number of changes that occurred over the period of one year, was unrelated to sex or age, but was associated to ethnicity [1]. The Irish showed the lowest level of stressful life events, while the Italians and the Polish showed relatively equal and higher stress levels. Social class was partialled out statistically; hence, reported differences in stress levels are not associated simply with the effect of social class differences among the three ethnic groups.

In examining the relationship between stress and adaptation, we found a positive association between level of stress characteristic of the three ethnic groups and frequency of successful adaptation. On a group basis, the Irish had the fewest number of malfunctioning (symptoms, depression, and anxiety) individuals, the Italians had more, and the Polish Americans had the most. This applied only to measures of breakdown, for all three groups were similar with regard to measures of well-being (LSI). On a macro-level, therefore, level of stress was associated with adaptation. So far, the analyses of data have suggested that stress plays an important role in affecting level of adaptation. A closer examination, however, indicates that the picture is more complex than so far portrayed. An examination of these relationships within specific ethnic groups indicates that among the Irish and the Polish, there was a modest relationship between stress and life satisfaction, but no association between stress and life satisfaction among the Italians. Over the age-span studied, some interesting relationships between stress and well-being appeared. Over the forty-year span represented by our population, women who reported high numbers of stressful life events experienced low levels of life satisfaction and, conversely, women with lower stress levels had high levels of life satisfaction. The relationships were more complex for men. For younger men, high levels of stress were associated with well-being; this relationship reversed itself in the sixties in which high levels of stress were associated with low levels of well-being; and, by the seventies, stress had no effect on life satisfaction levels.

Did the effect which stage of life and ethnicity have on mediating the relationship between stress and adaptation lie in the method used to assess stress? Were there changes in the meanings attributed to the scale items at different stages in the life cycle or by the different cultural groups? Previous research on the effects of cultural differences on the life stress index would not suggest large modifications in intensity rating of items [2]. Could the answer lie in the attitudes both the elderly men and the Italians had towards life events? The absence of a relationship between stress and well-being among these groups may have been caused by both being accustomed to, and perhaps anticipating, hardships, so that the actual occurrence of the "stress" event did not, in and of itself, lead to alteration of well-being. The unique personality constellation characteristic of the Italians studied indicated a paranoid mistrustful stance which was reflected in a fatalistic view of life and the anticipation of trouble. There is some suggestion from our study, as well as from other investigators looking at life span trajectories, that a similar personality profile may characterize aged men [3].

This particular speculation about factors that mediate the relationship between culture and age on stress is not as critical as is the observation that the re-thinking of such a relationship is in order. The reported findings that both culture and life stage (at least for men) affect this relationship demands entry into more complex models. The remainder of this paper will examine the base for such a model by contrasting the effects of personality and social surround on level of adaptation.

THE COMPARATIVE POWER OF PERSONALITY
AND SOCIAL SURROUND IN PREDICTION

What characteristics of a person—his relatively enduring personality qualities, crisis management techniques, views of social world and attitudes towards it, subjective and private symbols about salient personal issues—as well as what characteristics of the person's social surround—status characteristics, social networks and their use as resources, imbeddedness in a homogeneous social network—are important in accounting for differences in levels of adaptation? Each area is multi-dimensional, requiring multivariate techniques to analyze relationships. Both regression techniques, treating adaptation as a continuous variable, and linear discriminate analysis, viewing adaptation as a categorical variable, were used to analyze our data. Overall, both statistical techniques yielded similar results, although the discriminant analysis technique was some-what more conservative for a sample of this size. Table 1 provides the summary information on these analyses (using well-being as the criterion of adaptation). For the sample as a whole, personality indices yielded a multiple r of .41 for level of well-being. This accounted for 17 per cent of the variance, in comparison to a multiple r of .27 or 7 per cent of the variance for social indices. Although much of the variance was unexplained, personality measures were more robustly associated with level of well-being than were social indices. We next computed a number of discriminant analyses by reorganizing the sample based on the three major structural characteristics: life stage, sex, and ethnic affiliation.

An examination of Table 1 suggests that:

1. psychological indices showed, under all three structural arrangements, considerably higher association with adaptation than did social indices; and
2. variance accounted for by both psychological and social indices was significantly increased in relationship to adaptation when the effects of age, sex, and ethnic affiliation were statistically considered.

Table 1. Per cent Variance in Predicting Well Being

	Personality indices		State indices		Social indices	
Total Sample	17%	(.41)[a]	19%	(.44)	07%	(.27)
Ethnicity	24%	(.49)	21%	(.46)	14%	(.38)
Sex	22%	(.47)	20%	(.45)	10%	(.32)
Age	29%	(.54)	21%	(.46)	15%	(.39)
Age/Sex	43%	(.66)	25%	(.50)	24%	(.49)
Age/Ethnicity	55%	(.74)	29%	(.54)	49%	(.67)

[a] Canonical correlation

These three structural characteristics of a population increased the homogeneity of the groups, yielding higher levels of relationship between both personality and social indices in relationship to well-being. As shown in Table 1, life stage, particularly in the personality area, was the most homogeneous grouping in relationship to well-being, ethnicity was next, and sex was the least homogeneous. The consistent superiority of personality compared to social indices was striking. Division of the sample according to age and ethnic affiliation yielded the highest predictability, a multiple r of .74 which accounted for 55 per cent of the variance.

Some Illustrative Findings

THE RELATIONSHIP BETWEEN SOCIAL SURROUND AND WELL-BEING

Family network—Women had significantly larger and more active contact with family networks than did the men. Significant differences were found among the three ethnic groups, with the Italians having the most extensive family network, and the Irish having the smallest.

Size of family network was associated with well-being for men, but not for women, and played a role for the Irish but not for the other two ethnic groups. For both men and for the Irish, the larger the family network, the higher the level of well-being. The effect was also age specific as extensive family networks were associated with well-being among the middle-aged, a relationship which totally disappears in old age.

Ethnicity played some role in mediating the effects of family network on adaptation. As might be anticipated, extensive family networks were characteristic of particular ethnic groups, but the size of the family network available to the person did not play a role in adaptation except at younger ages. Although women had large family networks available to them, large family networks were negatively associated with well-being for women, particularly during middle age. Although men generally had smaller family networks, men with larger family networks were well off compared to the women. The availability of resources in and of itself was not a uniform predictor of well-being, but interacted primarily with age and sex and to some extent ethnicity.

A model based upon the relationship of kinship networks to adaptation, at least among these three groups studied in an urban setting, cannot be generalized beyond the bounds of a particular age/sex/ethnic configuration.

Ethnic homogeneity—This assesses the degree to which people live in a social surround that is ethnically consistent. Large differences were found among the three ethnic groups, with the Italians residing in the most ethnically homogeneous neighborhoods and the Polish in the least. There was an increased likelihood with increasing age for men to live in ethnically consistent neighborhoods. Ethnic homogeneity appeared important in affecting adaptation among aged men. There was not a clear-cut age-related living pattern among women. Sixty-year-old women who lived in ethnically homogeneous neighborhoods tended to be among the less adapted. The effect of ethnic homogeneity among men appeared to be particularly salient for the Polish and the Italians. The most consistent generalization is that it was more likely for women who resided outside ethnically homogeneous neighborhoods to have high LSI and for men, particularly among the oldest, who lived in ethnically consistent neighborhoods to have high LSI. Overall, in middle age, ethnic homogeneity was less important in affecting adaptation; it played a role in old age, but one that tended to be generally reversed for men and women.

THE RELATIONSHIP OF PERSONALITY TO WELL-BEING

Although there is some evidence from the study that ethnic affiliation is associated with particular personality characteristics, the relationships are neither clear-cut nor easily interpretable. More impressive is the association of ethnic homogeneity with unique personality characteristics that mediate adaptation. (The maximum multiple correlation obtained was .41 in associating ethnicity with personality in contrast to .74 when relating well-being to personality characteristics within the three cultures. Personality indices accounted for 16 per cent of the variance in differentiating among members of the three ethnic groups; predictions of well-being using personality variables within the same groups accounted for 55 per cent of the variance.)

For example, here is an illustration: authoritarianism sharply delineated the three ethnic groups. It was a dominant characteristic of the Polish, highly uncharacteristic of the Italians. An examination of the relationship of authoritarianism to adaptation reveals that, in general, the Polish who had high levels of authoritarianism had higher LSI. This relationship was reversed in the other ethnic groups where high levels of authoritarianism were associated with low levels of well-being. Differences between ethnic groups were more marked during middle age than among the elderly. For both the Italians and the Irish in the forties and fifties, low authoritarianism was associated with successful adaptation. For the Polish, authoritarianism was positively associated with well-being across the four age cohorts. However, among the Irish and Italian elderly, the relationship between authoritarianism and well-being reversed itself. In the sixties and seventies, high levels of authoritarianism among members of these two ethnic groups were associated with successful adaptation which was completely opposite to the findings for these ethnic groups in middle age.

An examination of sex differences on authoritarianism suggests some interesting patterns. Although women were generally lower on this trait, over the forty-year span studied, well-adapted women increased in authoritarianism and resembled the pattern characteristic of men; a trajectory that was not true of the low-adapted women who decreased in authoritarianism over the life span.

The analysis of a particular personality trait revealed several relationship sets of culture and life stage that mediated between personality and adaptation. A trait that characterized a particular cultural group is, within that group, adaptive. The Polish were highest in authoritarianism, and those who were higher in this trait among the Polish were more likely to have more successful adaptation than those who were lower in this trait. There were, however, salient age trajectories that need to be examined with regard to specific cultures. Authoritarianism was not characteristic of the Italians studied. During middle age, such traits were associated with the nonadapted Italians and Irish, although in both groups, adapted elderly were high on this trait.

Findings such as these, repeated in a number of personality indices examined, suggest a direction of understanding such as the one proposed by Gutmann [3] of personality trajectories over the life span. Gutmann suggests that as males age they become less agentic and more communion oriented, a direction that is reversed for women over the life span. We examined our personality data in light of Gutmann's hypothesis and found a number of these measures parallel his age trajectories for men and women. More important, however, is the finding that males who were deviant to these age trajectories were the ones who were most likely to be successful in adaptation than those who followed the age trajectories. Men who maintained a dominant, aggressive stance, such as authoritarianism, were most successful in old age. For women, the reverse was true. Women who matched the age trajectories suggested by Gutmann, who became more agentic with age (and in this sense resembled successful elderly males), were successful. The age changes suggested by Gutmann for women were only characteristic in our sample of women who had high levels of well-being.

These observations suggest an intriguing hypothesis. In middle age (and perhaps in younger age groups), culture may play a dominant role in mediating and providing pathways for personality constellations that are likely to be successful. However, life stage, regardless of culture, may play a more important function than culture among the elderly. This may be simply restating a survival hypothesis: particular personality traits, which have previously been suggested by several investigators to be survival oriented, are transcultural [3, 4].

Conclusions

The maze of relationships provided by these examples should amply demonstrate what Table 1 portrayed in an abstract way. No simple theoretical structure regarding the relationships among either psychological or social variables and well-being is likely to emerge. Life stage and cultural affiliation appear to be major mediators which must be considered before a reasonable model for understanding adaptation can be constructed.

Are the findings reported on the relationships among personality parameters, social characteristics, level of stress, and adaptation simply the product of a particular empirical study? I believe not. An examination of available studies reporting on the relationships between social parameters and well-being is revealing. Fundamental in these reports are investigators' assumptions about appropriate canons of evidence. The criteria used in this present study was the amount of variance explained by sets of variables. Other investigators have emphasized different conditions for acceptable evidence. For example, the oft-cited finding of an association between social class and mental health is underscored by investigators who are willing to accept relatively modest associations (in the case of social class and mental health, .2 correlations) in favor of other considerations. For those investigators, the repetition of such a finding from study to study and the web of theory spun around social class has become salient criteria for acceptable evidence.

An inter-related issue concerns the distinction between group characteristics and criterion variables compared to analysis of similar data which emphasized individual differences. In our own research, it was possible to order the three ethnic groups studied on a combination of social indices and to relate this to the number of members within each of these groups who were maladapted. In this light, our information mirrors other investigators' findings about the relationship of social characteristics to mental health. But, analyzing our data with the criterion amount of variance explained, our findings are often at odds, and more frequently yield results indicating that the statement is true for some groups of people at some points in the life span.

To what extent are the results which reported higher yields for personality compared to social surround indices an artifact of the criterion used to measure adaptation, a psychological variable? There is no adequate answer to this. However, some observations on the data may serve to counteract the artifactual possibilities. Similar multivariate statistical procedures to those used in portraying the findings reported on personality and social surround were used in analyzing the relationship between psychological state indices (e.g., anxiety and depression) and well-being. Such psychological variables are theoretically more similar to well-being than to the psychological trait and process indices. Despite this, the amount of variance accounted for by state variables was: 19 per cent for the total sample; for ethnicity, 21 per cent; for sex, 20 per cent; for age, 21 per cent; for age/sex, 25 per cent; and for age/ethnicity, 29 per cent. A comparison with Table 1 shows that these variances are considerably smaller than those for the personality indices.

Perhaps because we were blessed, or plagued, with an inquiry that used measures drawn from several frameworks, our evidence and modes of analysis suggest that a reasonable accounting for level of adaptation required a more complex accounting. The use of a survey research methodology with an emphasis on psychological as well as social-structural variables generates a much more complex model of adaptation. The findings suggest that considerable modifications are required in the standard explanations of well-being. Our understanding of the specific contribution of both ethnicity and life stage is far from complete at this point, and we can only offer suggestive speculations. But what is quite clear in our data is that simple relationships between person and social characteristics will not explain well-being. Even low order empirical generalizations seem hard to isolate. A good example is the relationship that we have observed between life stress and well-being, an oft-cited finding. This relationship held in some ethnic groups, yet not in others. To cite another example, social conditions that are theoretically associated with the maintenance of role behavior, such as social homogeneity, played a different role at different stages of life, as well as for different ethnic groups. On a macro-level, the generalizations found by other investigators do occur in our data; but as general truths, they do not portray magnitudes of relationships that many of us would be willing to accept as a source of explanation. Our results would also suggest that a strict personality position emphasizing intrinsic processes over the life span, a position that certainly has not been a popular one in the personality field during the past ten years, still merits consideration. To explain adaptation, such a model may prove to be more fruitful than models using social characteristics as their primary explanatory framework.

REFERENCES

1. E. S. Paykel and E. H. Uhlenhuth, Scaling of Life Events, *Archives of General Psychiatry, 25*, pp. 340-347, 1971.
2. B. S. Dohrenwend and B. Dohrenwend, *Stressful Life Events,* Wiley, New York, 1974.
3. D. Gutmann, *The Country of Old Men,* Institute of Gerontology, University of Michigan, Ann Arbor, 1969.
4. M. A. Lieberman, Adaptive Processes in Late Life, *Life-Span Developmental Psychology: Normative Life Crises,* N. Datan and L. Ginsberg, (eds.), Academic Press, New York, 1975.

part two

HOW DO WE
PERCEIVE AGE

chapter 4

TRANSITION TO AGING AND THE SELF-IMAGE[1]

Kurt W. Back

Research on aging has shown important contrasts between objective social and behavioral changes and the individual's reaction to them. Faculties and abilities as well as social rewards and objective social conditions decline rather consistently during the later years of the life cycle. On the other hand, subjective satisfaction and morale not only do not decrease correspondingly but seem to improve during old age (Riley and Foner, 1968; Back and Gergen, 1966). It is plausible to explain this apparent contradiction by the fact that morale is a personal comparison of self-worth with a realization of loss of socially important roles. While the loss itself may be traumatic, the new status may be acceptable later; for the aged, even social losses might be welcome adaptations to reduced capacity. It might be conjectured that physical capacity and energy decline steadily from early middle age on, while *psychological extent*, the size of the psychological life space, is maintained until a relatively sudden decline sets in at a comparatively late date. Thus, in early middle age we would find conformity between age and ability. During onset of old age, psychological extent would remain higher than actual life situation. But as psychological life space declines, the two would be rejoined again, and a high level of satisfaction is attained again (Back and Gergen, 1968).

Theoretical advance in this field must await measurement techniques that capture the personal meaning of the self concept. We are seeking a measure not of morale in the general sense, but of evaluation of the self, the discrepancy of the self-image one holds to the way one feels he is seen by others, and the different features of the self-image which may become important. The present paper deals with the evaluation of two possible measures of self-image: one an adaptation of the semantic differential, and the other an adaptation of Kuhn's Who-Are-You test (Kuhn and McPartland, 1954). These measures had been used previously to show not only the dimensions of the self-image but also the discrepancy between ideal, real, and actual self-image and self-presentation (Brehm and Back, 1968; Back and Paramesh, 1969).

The utility of these measures can be determined by their sensitivity to adaptation to aging of varying population groups, especially those with different problems during the aging process. Among the crises which can occur during the later parts of the life cycle, some appear in almost every life. One is the loss of occupational role through voluntary

[1] An earlier version of this paper was presented at the annual meeting of the American Gerontological Association in Toronto, Canada, October, 1970. This study was supported in part by Research Grant HD 0068 NICHD to the Center for the Study of Aging and Human Development, Duke University. We wish to acknowledge counsel and assistance from North Carolina Blue Cross and Blue Shield on statistical aspects of this study. The author thanks Mrs. Joanna Morris for invaluable assistance in analysis of the data.

or forced retirement; another, the loss of family role through the leaving home of grown children—the "empty nest" stage of the family sociologist. It can be suggested that the first crisis is of particular importance to men, while the second is of greater importance to women. A valuable use of the measures of self which we are trying to develop is therefore to assess the relative impact of chronological age, retirement, and leaving of children on men and women.

METHOD

The data to be reported here were collected as part of a future panel study on adaptation and aging to be conducted at the Duke Center for the Study of Aging and Human Development. The information collection involved a lengthy physical, physiological, psychological, and social assessment, lasting an entire day. The sample was designed to represent the wide middle class population. The intent was to draw an equal sample of men and women in each five-year range from 45 to 70, with some oversampling of the older ages to compensate for the higher expected loss in these age ranges during the life of the panel. The present data are based on the first wave of study in which 502 interviews were collected. This sample was a stratified random sample taken from the files of a major local health insurance company, stratified by sex and age. Refusals to be interviewed were replaced by substitutions from the same group. Almost half of the sample could not be interviewed on the first attempt and had to be substituted, partly because of the time-consuming and arduous medical procedures. The total sample actually interviewed did not differ in main social characteristics from the originally selected sample. But there is a possible bias in the direction of respondents more ready to cooperate with scientific research and less anxious about medical examination. In general, the method of selection would also oversample working women, which was fortunate for the present study.

The questions used in this paper were part of the social history section of the study. Social history gave age, sex, working status, and family situation, including separation from children. The measures of self-orientation were of two kinds: one was a semantic differential and the other the Who-Are-You test. The semantic differential consisted of a list of seven bipolar scales, each scored from one to seven, each of which rated three concepts. The concepts were, "What I really am"; "What I would like to be"; and "How I appear to others." The seven scales were, "useful, busy, effective, free to do things, respected, looking to the future, and satisfied with life." The first three (busy, effective, and useful) can be characterized as involvement, the last three (respected, looking to the future, and satisfied with life) as evaluation. Several different measures of the three concepts could be obtained from the twenty-one scales. One measure, the direct rating, could be used on each of the concepts, evaluation of self, ideal self, and self-presentation, along the seven dimensions. Second, on each of the dimensions, differences could be shown between members of each pair of the three concepts. Thus, for instance, we could determine whether the person felt he was more or less busy than he would like to be. Third, the overall difference between members of each pair of the three concepts could be computed. This was done by the difference formula suggested by Osgood, Tannenbaum and Suci (1957), which is the square root of the sums of the squared differences of all the seven scales. It can be visualized as a simple geometrical distance in a dimensional space. We shall be concerned here with the difference between the "real self" and "how I appear to others," the reality-appearance difference.

The Who-Are-You test is simply an open-ended rating of the self: "If someone were to ask you, 'Who are you?' what would you say?" The respondent himself can fill in all the dimensions which he likes and which seem to be important. The answers were scored in three main categories: (a) answers referring to *personal background*, family situation, ancestry, ethnic or religious identification, i.e. ascribed characteristics; (b) *personal characteristics* such as character, ambition, occupation; and (c) *personal values* such as beliefs, opinions, and attitudes. These three categories represent Riesman's classifications into other directed, inner directed, and traditionally oriented character structure (Riesman, Denny, and Glazer, 1950; Back and Paramesh, 1969). Each respondent gave three answers to the question, so that when the answers were combined, each of the three variables (personal background, personal characteristics, and personal values) had a possible range from zero to three. If a person gave three personal background items, he would be given a score of three on this variable and zero on the other two. If he listed two personal characteristics and one value, he would be scored two on characteristics and one on value. Here again, we can use the scores for each question as a basis of self-determination of the relevant variables of the self.

We have thus two ways of measuring the self-concept: (a) a qualitative self-anchored way, which lets the respondent choose the variables which he finds critical; (b) a measure based on a predetermined set of scales, which makes mathematical transformations possible.

RESULTS

Real Self versus Apparent Self

Let us look at one of the crises of the self-image occurring in aging—the contrast between what a person really feels about himself and the image that he presents to others. This is expressed by the difference between the semantic differential measures of the two concepts, the real self and the apparent self. An analysis of the distance measure between the two concepts, classified by sex and five-year age categories, shows significant differences by age, especially among women, although not in a monotonically increasing fashion. For women, the largest divergence between self and appearance of self occurs in the two oldest groups (60 to 64 and 65 and over), but the next is in the youngest group (45 to 49), followed by the other two groups (50 to 54 and 55 to 59). Among men, the sequence is almost regular, increasing with age, the only exception being a large difference in the 50 to 54 group. This sequence would indicate that the discrepancy is not due to an intrinsic effect of aging but to events in the life cycle which change the position of a person in the world.

There are two ways to learn more about the meaning of this changing reality-appearance contrast. One is by investigating the components and qualities which make up the self-image; the other is by comparing the reactions to the different crises of the later years. First, let us examine the semantic differential itself to determine which scales contribute most to the reality-appearance difference. Dividing the scales into three groups, involvement (busy, useful, and effective), evaluation (looks to future, satisfied, and respected), and freedom to do things (Guptill, 1969), only the involvement factor distinguished significantly between age groups, but this was affected by the sex of the respondent; the differences of the men were almost in the same order as the total

TABLE 1
Distance Between Apparent and Real Self
(Semantic Differential) by Sex and Age

	Under 50	50-54	55-59	60-64	65 and Over
Male	2.38	2.88	2.46	3.02	3.25
Female	2.64	2.59	2.49	2.69	2.92

Sex: $F(1,489) = 1.09$ n.s.
Age: $F(4,489) = 3.32$ $p < .05$
Sex x Age: $F(4,489) = .94$ n.s.

difference; among women the youngest group (45 to 49) had the greatest difference, then the oldest, and then the intermediate groups. Overall, the interaction between sex and age was statistically significant.

Going beyond the semantic differential itself, we can find some clues to the meaning of the reality-appearance difference in the answers to the Who-Are-You question. The strongest difference is revealed in the personal background directed answers. When asked who they are, women, in general, gave more answers relating to personal background, but this *declines* with age; men give fewer answers regarding personal background and their scores remain constant over the years; thus there is a great difference between the sexes in the youngest age group but none in the oldest group. Among women, therefore, personal background characteristics, which include family relations, become of diminishing importance with age.

Children Leaving Home

Because of the sex differences in the influence of age on the reality-appearance discrepancy, we shall investigate the particular crises which may affect the sexes differently using the semantic differential. Let us examine first the departure from home of the children. Controlling for this variable we find age differences only in men. In other words, the age difference in the discrepancy of the real self and appearance to others is due mainly to the departure of the children among women, but not among men.

The influence of age on the reality-appearance difference among women is thus partially accounted for by the fact that older women have fewer children living at home. Child separation, however, does not affect age changes in the interpretation of the meaning of the self. In response to the Who-Are-You question, the shift among women from personal background to achieved traits becomes stronger if controlled for child separation. Among men there is little change in the Who-Are-You question, while among women there is a sharp decline of personal background items by age and an increase in value items with age in each group, classified according to child separation.

Retirement

By contrast, work and retirement affect both sexes in the same manner. Controlling for work status, we find no more differences according to age, but definite differences by sex and work status: men and non-workers claim the bigger difference between appearance and reality of the self-image. Looking at the Who-Are-You question we can

TABLE 2

Difference of Three Scale Clusters Between Apparent and Real Self
by Sex and Age

	Involvement		Evaluation		Freedom	
	Male	Female	Male	Female	Male	Female
Under 50	.11	.19	.30	−.01	−.09	−.16
50-54	.28	.02	.12	.11	.19	−.43
55-59	.25	.26	.33	.22	.32	−.04
60-64	.36	.10	.35	.15	−.11	−.04
65 and over	.09	.32	.32	.35	.32	−.24
Sex $F(1,492)$	.39 n.s.		3.82 $p < .10$		4.77 $p < .05$	
Age $F(4,492)$	.42 n.s.		1.73 n.s.		.55 n.s.	
Sex x Age $F(4,492)$	2.25 $p < .10$		1.08 n.s.		.89 n.s.	

TABLE 3

Who-Are-You Score by Age and Sex

	Personal Background		Personal Characteristics		Values	
	Male	Female	Male	Female	Male	Female
Under 50	.43	1.35	1.09	1.00	1.00	.23
50-54	.53	.98	1.16	1.27	.86	.61
55-59	.57	.81	1.02	1.00	.73	.71
60-64	.38	.67	1.40	1.20	.78	.70
65 and over	.39	.41	1.27	1.13	.85	.94
Sex $F(1,492)$	24.82 $p < .01$		.56 n.s.		6.67 $p < .05$	
Age $F(4,492)$	5.00 $p < .01$		1.55 n.s.		1.29 n.s.	
Sex x Age $F(4,492)$	3.81 $p < .01$		.37 n.s.		3.60 $p < .01$	

TABLE 4

Distance Between Apparent and Real Self by Sex, Age
and Children's Residence (Parents Only)

	Male		Female	
	Children Not at Home	Children At Home	Children Not at Home	Children At Home
Under 50	1.92	2.43	2.83	2.64
50-54	2.45	3.21	2.40	2.67
55-59	2.33	2.37	2.29	2.43
60-64	2.95	3.33	2.66	2.18
65 and over	3.30	3.54	2.96	2.57

Sex $F(1,402) = 1.97$ n.s.
Age $F(4,402) = 2.68$ $p < .05$
Child Residence $F(1,402) = .64$ n.s.
Sex x Age $F(4,402) = 2.20$ $p < .10$
Other interactions not significant

TABLE 5
Who-Are-You Score by Age, Sex and Children's Residence
(Parents Only)

	A. Personal Background			
	Male		Female	
	Children Not at Home	Children At Home	Children Not at Home	Children At Home
Under 50	.38	.46	1.13	1.63
50-54	.50	.60	1.10	1.11
55-59	.53	.75	.81	.73
60-64	.35	.63	.75	1.29
65 and over	.43	.45	.51	0.00

Sex $F(1,404) = 14.88$ p $< .01$
Age $F(4,404) = 3.41$ p $< .01$
Child Residence $F(1,404) = 1.26$ n.s.
Sex x Age $F(4,404) = 3.61$ p $< .01$
Other interactions not significant

	B. Personal Characteristics			
Under 50	1.00	1.08	1.50	.68
50-54	1.36	1.08	1.10	1.32
55-59	1.11	1.06	.88	1.36
60-64	1.32	1.25	1.21	.57
65 and over	1.28	1.36	1.13	.80

No significant F ratios

	C. Values			
Under 50	1.23	.92	.13	.21
50-54	.93	.72	.70	.37
55-59	.74	.94	.75	.73
60-64	.91	.38	.71	.86
65 and over	.85	.73	.85	2.00

Sex $F(1,404) = 1.04$ n.s.
Age $F(4,404) = 2.71$ p $< .05$
Child Residence $F(1,404) = 0.00$ n.s.
Sex x Age $F(4,404) = 6.05$ p $< .01$
Sex x Child $F(1,404) = 3.84$ p $\sim .05$
Other interactions not significant

see the traits that may account for these differences. Among the retirees, women mention significantly more personal background data and men more individual characteristics. Among the workers there is no difference in amount of personal background data, but women mention more individual characteristics.

In order to assess the relative importance of separation from work and child, we have to control simultaneously for work and family status. Because there are too few male non-workers in the younger ages, we cannot control for both in the whole age range. Instead we can measure the influence of child separation in the working respondents in this group: for men the reality-appearance discrepancy increases with age, and for women it declines; further, for men the discrepancy increases with child separation, and for

TABLE 6

Distance Between Apparent and Real Self by Age,
Sex and Work Status

	Male		Female	
	Working	Not Working	Working	Not Working
Under 60	2.55	2.71	2.62	2.45
60-65	2.91	3.14	2.49	2.69
Over 65	3.23	3.56	1.92	3.29

Sex $F(1,487) = 7.00$ p $< .01$
Age $F(2,487) = 2.07$ n.s.
Work $F(1,487) = 4.51$ p $< .05$
Age x Work $F(2,487) = 2.35$ p $< .10$
Other interactions not significant

TABLE 7

Who-Are-You Score by Age, Sex, and Work Status

A. Personal Background

	Male		Female	
	Working	Not Working	Working	Not Working
Under 60	.54	2.00	.88	1.20
60-65	.36	.20	.59	.67
Over 65	.59	.30	.42	.40

Sex $F(1,490) = 11.63$ p $< .01$
Age $F(2,490) = 1.91$ n.s.
Work $F(1,490) = .92$ n.s.
Sex x Age $F(2,490) = 4.92$ p $< .01$
Sex x Work $F(1,490) = 4.74$ p $< .05$
Other interactions not significant

B. Personal Characteristics

Under 60	1.07	1.57	1.26	.84
60-65	1.41	1.60	1.47	.97
Over 65	1.07	1.30	1.33	1.06

Sex $F(1,490) = 2.33$ n.s.
Age $F(2,490) = .95$ n.s.
Work $F(1,490) = .13$ n.s.
Sex x Work $F(1,490) = 8.33$ p $< .01$
Other interactions not significant

C. Values

Under 60	.82	.71	.56	.50
60-65	.82	.70	.76	.93
Over 65	1.03	.79	.92	.90

No significant F ratios

TABLE 8
Distance Between Apparent and Real Self
by Age, Sex, and Children's Residence
(Working Only, Parents Only)

	Male		Female	
	Children Not at Home	Children At Home	Children Not at Home	Children At Home
Under 50	1.92	2.43	3.24	2.62
50-54	2.45	3.21	2.29	2.49
55-59	2.30	2.37	2.62	2.61
60-64	3.03	3.16	2.13	1.38
65 and over	2.77	4.41	1.94	1.71

Sex $F(1,265) = 6.76 \; p < .01$
Age $F(4,265) = .26$ n.s.
Child Residence $F(1,265) = .78$ n.s.
Sex x Age $F(4,265) = 5.99 \; p < .01$
Sex x Child $F(1,265) = 5.43 \; p < .05$
Other interactions not significant

women it declines. There are no significant differences according to the Who-Are-You question.

DISCUSSION

The data presented here have shown the values and limitations of the two measures which we have employed in studying the changes in self-concept brought on by old age. The most consistent result has been the sex differences in the answers to the Who-Are-You question. Women are more likely to answer in terms of personal background, such as family relations and demographic characteristics, but this emphasis declines after the fifties such that in the last age groups, 60 to 64 and 65 and over, there is no difference between the sexes in this regard. Correspondingly, personally achieved positions and characteristics, as well as personal values, become more important for women with age. This development remains constant even if controlled for varying experiences, such as retirement and child separation during aging.

Thus, neither retirement nor separation from children affects the content of the self-image as much as the aging process alone. However, the discrepancy between reality and appearance of the self is influenced by these factors. Both crises are important; but separation from children accounts only for the effect on women, while retirement or non-working affects both sexes. In general, men have a greater problem with the discrepancy between who they feel they are and what they imagine other people think about them. This is also true with non-working members of both sexes.

During the aging process, women tend to shift their self-image from their relationship to others, the social characteristics, to their own abilities and feelings; the separation from children can be viewed in this way. Freed from family obligations, they may feel that they can now much more easily be accepted for what they are. Men, on the other hand, are involved in the work role more personally, and difficulties with this role through aging may make life even more difficult for them. Separation from children may, therefore, aggravate this discrepancy, making them more dependent on the work role in which they have difficulty in presenting the right image. Hence the increase in self-image discrepancy in working men separated from children, while for women the discrepancy decreases with age and separation from children.

Measures of the self-image that can be administered in a relatively simple manner to a large sample can show some of the more subtle features of the management of crises incumbent on the aged.

REFERENCES

Back, K. W., & Gergen, K. J. Personal orientation and morale of the aging. In J. McKinney & I. Simpson (Eds.), *Social aspects of aging*. Durham, N. C.: Duke University Press, 1966.

Back, K. W., & Gergen, K. J. The self through the latter span of life. In C. Gordon and K. J. Gergen (Eds.), *The self in social interaction*. New York: Wiley, 1968.

Back, K. W., & Paramesh, C. R. Self-image, information exchange and social character. *International Journal of Psychology*, 1969, *4*, 109-117.

Brehm, M. L., & Back, K. W. Self image and attitude toward drugs. *Journal of Personality*, 1968, *35*, 299-314.

Guptill, C. S. A measure of age identification. *Gerontologist*, 1969, *9* (Summer), 96-102.

Kuhn, M. H., & McPartland, T. S. An empirical investigation of self-attitudes. *American Sociological Review*, 1954, *19*, 68-76.

Osgood, C., Suci, G. and Tannenbaum, P. *The measurement of meaning*. Urbana, Ill.: University of Illinois Press, 1957.

Riesman, D., Denny, R., & Glazer, N. *The lonely crowd*. New Haven: Yale University Press, 1950.

Riley, M. W., & Foner, A. *Aging and society, vol. I: An inventory of research findings*. New York: Russell Sage Foundation, 1968.

chapter 5

THE MEASUREMENT OF SOCIAL AGE[1]

Charles L. Rose, Ph.D.

INTRODUCTION

The sociology of aging is a burgeoning field responding to the dramatic increase in longevity in the past half century and the related increase in percent of population in older age groupings. The new field has encompassed the use of demographic concepts and social change concepts. Interventional and organizational concepts have also been used to assuage the problems of older people. Finally, the role concept has been utilized in understanding the process of social aging and adjustment to aging.

This paper proposes an additional concept and technique for the sociology of aging, that of *social age* and its measurement. The usefulness of the concept is demonstrated in the context of other domains of functional age. A specific example is presented from data of the Normative Aging Study (Bell, et al., 1966).

Social age is defined conceptually as a changing composite of social life styles, attributes, and attitudes at various points of the life cycle. Technically, it is defined as the predicted age yielded by a multiple regression equation composed of weighted social variables and a constant. Individuals whose social life styles are the same as those of their age peers would have a social age the same as their chronological age. If their life styles are more characteristic of those found in older individuals, their social age would be higher than their chronological age, and vice versa. The relationship between the technical and conceptual definitions will be clarified as the argument of this paper is developed.

Social age is not the equivalent of chronological age, since the social universe exists *sui generis,* and in fact refers to only one sector of reality, or one way of looking at reality. Social age is therefore a special case of a larger concept of functional age, which is different from chronological age. Just as an individual may be younger or older in the way he functions socially, so he may also have a psychological or physiological functional age. An individual may be old in years and have a young personality, or vice versa; an old individual may have a young heart or a young person who imbibes too

55

much may have an old liver. Thus, one might conceptualize functional age as different from chronological age, with all sorts of sectors of functional age—social, psychological, biological, and so on. Clearly, functional age more accurately depicts the individual than does his chronological age. Chronological age at best is an approximation of functional age at the individual level.

The concept of functional age is not entirely new. Heron and Chown (1967) developed profiles of psychological functioning, relating means to various age levels. These graded values of the psychological measures were referred to as the functional age in the psychological sector. Developmental psychologists developed the IQ on the basis of the concept of mental age, which is the functional age in the area of intellectual functioning. Age norms developed in medicine with respect to various organ systems also embody the functional age idea. Birren (1959) specifically conceptualized social age, but defined it narrowly in terms of adequacy of social role performance.

The advance in the measurement of social age lies in the use of multiple regression analysis and in the exploitation of the comprehensive multidisciplinary data of the Normative Aging Study. The combination of an expanded independent variable set and multivariate analysis makes possible a better development and application of the concept. The specific opportunities for analysis and theory building are presented below and are further illustrated in the data example.

Uses of the Social Age Measure

(1) A multiple regression equation treats the predictor set as one variable and encourages the treatment of the ingredients of social age as a unitary system. In addition, the stepwise multiple regression technique facilitates the study of the anatomy of this system, as the system is experimentally changed through the stepwise addition of independent variables. Since the elements of the system are interrelated either by partial redundancies or other special effects, these relationships may be evaluated during the evolution of the stepwise procedure.

(2) Related to the above is the opportunity to assess the relative importance of the independent variables. As will be seen in the example below, more than half the variables inserted into the procedure were found to contribute negligibly to social age, and of those that did contribute significantly, the relative importance of each was quantitatively specified. This suggests a causal model which can be tested by regressing specific variables on other variables in the test or some equivalent procedure such as path analysis. The upshot is the possibility for building a general model of social age, which will have implications both for understanding the role of aging in the society and the consequences for individual experience.

A caveat is needed in connection with the construction of this model. The variables selected for consideration will influence the final composition of the model. Since initial selection requires an initial model of sorts, the initial model will influence the resulting model. In addition, alternative variable sets based even on the same initial model will influence the results. The experimentation with various variable sets will not merely shed light on the best model but also on the relationships among alternative initial models which may be tried. In view of such considerations, a particular equation is not the magical answer to social age. It is a possible embodiment of the concept, one to be further assessed for its usefulness.

(3) The independent variable set in the regression procedure can be expanded by insertion of other domains of variables. These additional domains may refer to other

functional ages, such as psychological, physiological, etc. This procedure enables examination of the linkages among the various domains of functional age and enables more general theoretical formulation than would be possible merely through within-domain analysis. Since aging is multi-faceted, a multi-domain functional age would better fit the overall phenomenon of functional age as distinct from chronological age.

The multi-domain functional age reveals what part social age plays in the larger functional age, or in a larger segment of functional age. For example, one can arrange a series of domains—social, personality, abilities, clinical measures, and biochemistry measures. In stepwise fashion one can then insert the first domain, then add the second, the third, etc., and at each step see how the functional age changes. This is similar to the stepwise analysis within domains but using the domain as the unit stepped in rather than the specific variable. For this domain-level stepwise procedure, one would first run the regressions within domains in order to identify the best variables of each, and then insert the reduced domain sets into the cross-domain procedure. This can be varied somewhat, depending upon the number of variables that can be accommodated by available computational power.

A social age score (in years) can be generated for each individual and can be compared to scores in other areas of functional age. Change in patterns of these scores for groups at different chronological ages would yield relative rates of aging of various areas of aging.

An overall functional age score can be obtained by multiple regression of chronological age on a set of independent variables including the most important variables obtained from within-domain age regressions. Social age, or any other domain of functional age, can then be related to the overall functional age. This would then allow social age to be studied in its larger context of aging in general.

The profiles of functional age would suggest what areas require interventional services. Changes in the profile over time would also monitor the effects of treatment.

(4) Consistency or inconsistency in within-domain measures at the individual level may be used to generate an additional variable which may be called *social age inconsistency,* which is analogous to the status inconsistency concept (Lenski, 1954). If an individual is high in one social indicator of age and low in another, he may be said to be social age inconsistent. The same thinking of course could be applied to other domains of functional age.

The same variable could also be generated across domains, so that older age in one domain and younger age in another may be considered *functional age inconsistency.* Such inconsistencies within domains or across domains, like status inconsistency, could be hypothesized to relate to all manner of problems, in this case, problems within the general field of aging adjustment. One example within the social age domain is the middle-aged person who has the fluid and unsettled occupational orientation of the young, but the diminished moving plans characteristic of the elderly. A cross-domain example is a person who is socially old (e.g., has a job with little chance for advancement) and clinically young (e.g., high level of pulmonary function).

(5) The sort of variables initially inserted into a social age determination should be variables which in fact vary with age. However, once equations yielding social age are generated, it would be important to learn whether subpopulations defined by age-invariant criteria differ with respect to social age. Such variations would give additional information on differential aging patterns and suggest the determinants of such differences. Again, the extent of cross-domain functional age as opposed to

specific within-domain functional age could well have an effect on whether there are subpopulation variations.

(6) A *functional age quotient* could be constructed, made up of functional age divided by chronological age. This quotient follows the model of the universal intelligence quotient, except that in the case of mental age there is supposedly no change after a certain fixed age. Functional age, on the other hand, changes throughout adulthood. A quotient could be constructed of social age divided by chronological age, or social age divided by overall functional age. The first would be a measure of the extent to which an individual is socially older or younger than his chronological age. The second would be a measure of the extent to which an individual is socially older or younger than his overall functional age. An alternative would be to subtract social age from chronological age, or overall functional age, as the case may be.

Secular Effect

In cross-sectional analysis, the dependent variable of the regression equation—chronological age—refers to members of different age cohorts. Differences in chronological age of a given population therefore leave wide open the possibility that the predictor variables reflect secular effects rather than, or in addition to, age change (Rose & Bell, 1971). An attempt was therefore made to restrict the predictor set to measures that did not obviously reflect secular change. A salient example is education. Because of the secular shift to education, a given population may well show a correlation between older age and less education, since the older subjects received their education when less education was available. However, this is obviously a secular rather than an age effect, since education once completed does not change with age.

A more precise way of controlling for secular effects is to investigate age-related functional changes by longitudinally following a given cohort. In this case, the dependent variable would be variation in chronological age at various points in time when functional change is recorded. For example, changes in job satisfaction, job mobility, and anything else could be related to age within such a longitudinal design. The difficulty with this approach is the time needed for the study. This tends to justify the cross-sectional design, cautiously used, and giving immediate results. However, the longitudinal design of the Normative Aging Study will, over time, provide the optimal method for developing functional age.

POPULATION ON WHICH
SOCIAL AGE WAS DEVELOPED

The population of the Normative Aging Study, consisting of over 2,000 healthy male veterans from the Boston area, was used to develop the social age equation. The chronological age range was 28 to 83, with 42 percent of the group in the age decade 40-49. Aside from this large modal group, the distribution was skewed to the younger range, with 35 percent under 40, 18 percent between 50 and 59, and only 5 percent age 60 and over. In addition, the population had special geographic stability characteristics required for their lifelong participation in the study. For example, 82 percent were born in the Boston area, 71 percent lived in a single dwelling, 92 percent were married, 84 percent had children of school age at home, and 80 percent planned to remain with their present job until retirement. Their educational level was higher than the general male population: 64 percent had some education beyond high school, of which 28 percent were college graduates.

In addition, the population was rigorously screened medically before being allowed to join the study. This was done because the overall research objective was to study aging in an initially healthy population, in order to understand aging as a process distinct from the development of disease. The result, however, was a population which was relatively homogeneous medically and socially. This provides a severe test for the emergence of statistically significant findings since variances are reduced

It could be argued quite correctly that findings from the Normative Aging population on social age or other areas of functional age cannot be universalized. However, they can be generalized to other populations of similar characteristics. Also, a major thrust of this paper is to test a method which is promising for constructing aging theory. Possibly the method can then be used on other populations. In all due fairness it should be added, in view of the constraints involved in using cross-sectional age for developing functional age, the Normative Aging Study population is more heterogeneous than other extant longitudinal aging study populations, and as such provides a good data basis for developing functional age through longitudinal analysis.

The present analysis is part of a larger functional age project in the Normative Aging Study, including other domains in psychology and medicine. The psychological data are on the 16 PF test (Cattell, et al., 1957), (Personality and abilities) and the GATB (Bureau of Employment Security, 1967). Since psychological data at the moment are available only on about half the population, the data presented are only on this subgroup, because of the need for a population on which all domains of data are available (N = 966). For the social and medical domains, data are available on the total population, so that in addition functional ages on these areas will be run on all cases. Findings from the total and reduced population can then be compared, to see whether stability of findings is maintained on a reduced population. In fact, the social age analysis on the larger population was done and produced results similar to those presented here.

MEASURES

The social measures were taken from the Social Screening Questionnaire which every subject filled out as part of the overall screening procedure set up to generate a pool of healthy and geographically stable subjects. Although the items included in the questionnaire were designed to test for geographic stability, the questionnaire also included general social data which had theoretic relevance for relationship to aging and other domains of the study. Out of this pool, variables were selected on which the basis of zero order correlations had some correlation with age. Twenty-four such independent variables were selected for insertion into a multiple regression procedure whose criterion was age as of time of entry into the study. The percentage age distribution by age decades of the 966 cases was as follows: under 30, 4.1 percent; 30 to 39, 35.1 percent; 40 to 49, 38.2 percent; 50 to 59, 18.3 percent; and 60 and over, 4.3 percent.

The 24 social variables were made up of 7 family variables, 13 occupational variables, 2 social class variables, and 2 health behavior variables. These variables, together with their zero order correlations with age, are shown in Table 1. It will be noted that some variables were included despite an insignificant r because of their theoretical interest such as frequency of going to a doctor and some of the job satisfaction variables. It should be kept in mind that interaction effects sometimes elevate the importance of a variable which has a low zero r, and if such variables were omitted they would not have a chance to show their greater importance in a multivariate framework. As it turned out, no variable with an r below .15 entered the resulting 10-variable regression equation.

METHOD OF ANALYSIS

The 24 variables were inserted into a stepwise multiple regression procedure with chronological age as dependent variable. To deal with missing observations, the method of pair-wise deletions was used. Under this method, correlations are computed only on those cases for which data are available on each pair of variables. The program steps in variables in order of highest partial r at that point in the procedure. Since the variance accounted for by each variable (R^2 change) is influenced by the order in which it is entered into the equation, the relative variance contributed by each variable was computed by the product of the beta weight and r (Hoffman, 1962). Another measure of relative importance of variables was obtained from the F value of each variable in the final model. Interactions among variables were examined by the evolution of F values during the stepwise procedure. Finally, some comparisons were made with regression results from psychological and biochemistry domains of variables.

TABLE 1

Social Variables Used for Determination of
Social Age and their Zero Order Correlations
with Chronological Age

	$r*$ with chronological age
Family Variables	
Geographic distance from S's relatives	.16
Geographic distance from wife's relatives	.12
Plans to relocate in next 10 years	.21
Number of contacts by S and wife with S's relatives	-.21
Number of contacts by S and wife with wife's relatives	-.23
Number of children in household	-.08
Wife's employment	.20
Occupational Variables	
Likelihood of remaining with company until retirement	.22
Higher self-ranking in hierarchy of company	.17
Self-rating re chances for advancement	-.29
Later age of expected retirement	.23
Later age of preferred retirement	.26
Satisfaction with job regarding:	
one's authority	.15
pressure	.07
initiative allowed	.06
salary	.15
opportunity for advancement	.01
one's supervisor	.07
job security	.08
overall satisfaction	.09
Social Class	
Warner S.E.S. level	.02
Single home residence	.12
Health-Behavior	
Frequency of going to a doctor in past year	.05
Frequency of going to a doctor for checkup in absence of illness	.10

* r of .08 and above of N of 966 is significant at $p < .01$, and .06 and above is significant at $p < .05$.

RESULTS OF STEPWISE REGRESSION OF
AGE ON SOCIAL VARIABLES

After 10 variables entered the equation, the R^2 was .355 and thereafter the R^2 change was less than .01 for any variable entered. When an additional 14 variables had been entered the R^2 had only risen to .373. Accordingly, the 10-variable equation was adopted as a significant set of predictors of chronological age.

Table 2 shows the ten variables ranked in order of *beta x r*. Since the sum of the (beta x r) is equal to R^2, (beta x r)/R^2 is the contribution of each variable to the accountable variance. These values are also shown in Table 2. Table 3 shows the differences in ranking of importance of variables by beta x r, order of selection (R^2 change), beta and *F*. Tables 4 and 5 show the evolution of *F* values during the stepwise procedure, indicating some of the special interactions among the variables.

Components of Social Age

The equation tells us that social age as measured by the 10 variables has a multiple correlation of .60 with chronological age. With this degree of relationship (or non-relationship) to chronological age, social age is made up of 6 occupational variables and 4 family variables. This proportion reflects the number of occupational variables

TABLE 2

Ten-Variable Regression Equation Predicting Age
from Social Variables

Variables ranked in order of beta x r	Relation to older age	Beta	r with age	Proportion of total variance (beta x r)	Proportion of accountable variance (beta x r)/R^2	F
1. Chances for advancement	Less	.283	.288	.081	.229	92.6
2. Remaining with company	More	.231	.216	.050	.140	63.4
3. Preferred retirement age	Later	.142	.257	.037	.103	16.9
4. Relocation plans	Less	.168	.214	.036	.010	33.9
5. Wife employed	More	.163	.201	.033	.092	32.1
6. Expected retirement age	Later	.135	.227	.031	.086	15.4
7. Contacts with wife's family	Less	-.130	-.228	.030	.084	17.4
8. Self-ranking in company	Higher	.139	.172	.024	.067	21.1
9. Contacts with S's family	Less	-.099	-.209	.021	.058	10.0
10. Satisfaction with salary	More	.092	.153	.014	.040	9.8

Constant 30.002
R (multiple correlation).5962
R^2 (Accountable variance).3555
S.E.7.346 years

(13) and family variables (7) in the total independent variable set inserted into the procedure. The importance of the occupational and family variables was roughly in proportion to their numbers in the equation. Thus, the 6 occupational variables accounted for 66.5 percent of the accountable variance while the 4 family variables accounted for the remainder, 33.5 percent. However, the occupational variables could be regarded as having somewhat of an edge, since the 3 most important variables, (in terms of beta x r) accounting for 47.2 percent of the accountable variance, were all occupational variables.

In order of importance, social age under the equation is determined by the following: 1) self-perceptions regarding fewer chances for occupational advancement, 2) self-perceptions regarding remaining longer with the company, 3) preference for later retirement, 4) less expectation for relocation, 5) wife being employed, 6) expectation of later retirement on realistic grounds, 7) fewer contacts with wife's family, 8) higher self-ranking in company, 9) fewer contacts with subject's family, and 10) more satisfaction with salary. Each of these is weighted (beta x r). For example, chances for advancement is weighted 3 times preferred retirement age, 4 times contacts with subject's family, and 5.7 times satisfaction with salary.

The overall picture can be seen more clearly if the lowest ranking, satisfaction with salary, is given a weight of 1, and the correspondingly higher weights on this basis are calculated for the other variables. This is shown below, with variables shown in order of increasing weights:

	Weight
Satisfaction with salary	1
Contacts with *S*'s family	
Self-ranking in company	1.7
Contacts with wife's family	2.1
Expected retirement age	2.2
Wife employed	2.3
Relocation plans	2.5
Preferred retirement age	2.6
Remaining with company	3.5
Chances for advancement	5.7

TABLE 3

Variables Ranked in Order of Importance by Hoffman Weight
(beta x r), as Compared to Rank by Variance Accounted for
(R^2 change), beta and F

	Beta x r	*R^2 change**	*Beta*	*F*
Chances for Advancement	1	1	1	1
Remaining with Company	2	3	2	2
Preferred Retirement	3	2	5	7
Relocation Plans	4	6	3	3
Wife's Employment	5	7	4	4
Expected Retirement	6	8	7	8
Contacts with Wife's family	7	5	8	6
Rank in Company	8	4	6	5
Contacts with *S*'s family	9	9	9	9
Satisfaction with Salary	10	10	10	10

*Corresponds to order in which variables were selected. Criterion for stepwise selection was highest partial r.

TABLE 4

Stepwise Evolution of F Values Before and After Selection*

Variables in order of selection	F Values at Various Steps in Procedure									
	1	2	3	4	5	6	7	8	9	10
1. Chances Advancement	72.0	76.4	88.3	110.8	105.7	99.3	94.8	95.9	92.3	92.6
2. Preferred Retirement	60.8	60.8	71.4	54.5	50.3	50.8	55.3	18.8	17.9	16.9
3. Remain in Company	48.7	59.1	59.1	64.7	65.9	66.6	63.5	67.6	70.3	63.4
4. Rank in Company	46.2	31.6	37.0	37.0	32.9	28.5	29.1	28.3	27.2	21.7
5. Contacts Wife's Family	40.9	35.2	36.7	32.5	32.5	37.5	33.9	34.6	18.1	17.4
6. Relocation Plans	34.4	34.2	35.0	30.8	35.8	35.8	35.6	34.6	35.0	33.9
7. Employment of Wife	29.5	34.8	31.8	32.3	29.0	28.8	28.8	30.3	30.4	32.1
8. Expected Retirement	46.3	9.7	13.4	12.5	13.3	12.4	13.9	13.9	13.5	15.4
9. Contacts S's Family	31.2	24.8	29.3	26.0	10.3	10.6	10.7	10.3	10.3	10.0
10. Satisfied with Salary	22.7	21.8	15.3	8.4	7.4	6.6	8.0	10.1	9.8	9.8

*F values before selection are below diagonal; F values after selection are above.

64 / CHARLES L. ROSE

TABLE 5

Initial F, Selection F, and Final F of Variables
in Age Regression Equation*

Variables in Order of Selection	Initial F	Selection F	Final F
1. Chances for Advancement	72.0	72.0	92.6
2. Preferred Retirement	60.8	60.8	16.9
3. Remain with Company	48.7	59.1	63.4
4. Rank in Company	46.2	37.0	21.7
5. Contacts with Wife's Family	40.9	32.5	17.4
6. Relocation Plans	34.4	35.8	11.9
7. Employment of Wife	29.5	28.8	32.1
8. Expected Retirement	46.3	13.9	15.4
9. Contacts with S's Family	31.2	10.3	10.0
10. Satisfaction with Salary	22.7	9.8	9.8

*Summarized from Table 4.

Aside from the weighting, the "sense" of the 10 descriptors of social age is as follows: An individual is older occupationally when he settles down to remain with the company until retirement, sees himself as having advanced in the company hierarchy, has come to terms with his salary level and consequently sees his future chances for advancement approaching an asymptote. In a word, his mobility aspirations decrease. This picture, interestingly, corresponds to the most important characteristic of psychological age, the factor of "surgency" as derived from an age regression on the 16 factors of Cattell's 16 PF test. One settles down as one gets older. An individual of whatever chronological age is young occupationally if he is still looking to change his job, sees advancement still ahead of him, etc.

With respect to the domestic area, an individual is old if he gives up or substantially reduces his future plans for relocating his household. This age-related geographic stability is related to the occupational stability described above. Thus, social age is characterized by engagement in community and occupational roles. Another sign is wife going to work. This can be understood in terms of reduction in parental role when the children get older. Another sign is the reduction in contacts with the kin network, including loss of parents and older siblings due to death. This refers to disengagement from matrilateral and patrilateral kin network.

Finally, an "old" perception of occupational retirement is to stave off retirement, consonant with increase in occupational engagement. A young person who dreads retirement may therefore be considered socially old, and an older person looking forward to an early retirement may be considered to be socially young. The inclination of younger people to perfer early retirement has been explained on the basis of youthful hedonism, and the fact that at an earlier age the work pattern has not yet become fully ingrained (Benge & Copell, 1947). It appears as if settling in the occupational role, as depicted above, makes it more difficult to relinquish it. Generally, when loss of occupational role is comfortably in the future, it can be countenanced more easily than when it is closer at hand. This increase in occupational engagement with age clearly conflicts with loss of occupational role through retirement. The problem thus created is the rationale for retirement preparation.

In summary, one is socially old before his time if, relative to the respective age norms, he is more settled in his job, staves off retirement, has a working wife, does not plan to relocate, and sees less of his relatives. At this point, no implication is intended as to the desirability or undesirability of being socially old.

Perceptions regarding future behavior emerge as the most important elements in social age. The four highest ranking variables are of this type: chances for advancement, remaining with company, preferred retirement age, and relocation plans. In the original 23 variables, 6 were linked to future behavior, while in the 10-variable equation 5 were of this type. In addition to being the most important in the equation they also had a better chance of getting into the equation. This suggests two things: 1) present status evaluated in terms of future expectation is a powerful index of age-related status, 2) age-related self-evaluations can be made reliably by a respondent.

The variable "age of expected retirement" is not entirely a measure involving age-related future orientation, since it is related to realities of the pension and retirement plan of one's job, and is to this extent invariant with age of subject. However, it did show a substantial relationship with age (r = .227) suggesting that older subjects tend to want to retire at the latest possible age allowed by their pension plan while younger subjects opt for an earlier retirement.

Figure 1 shows the change in mean values of 4 selected predictors across 10-year age groups. For comparability, the mean values are presented in standardized units. Decrease in self-perceived chances for advancement takes place particularly between the fourth and fifth decade. The increase in wife's employment and decrease in contacts with relatives are fairly linear over the age range. The older preferred retirement age is expressed particularly after age 50. The curve also shows that those under 30 are more like the 50-59 age group than the 30-49 group. From this it may be speculated that those who have just entered the occupational role are more sanguine

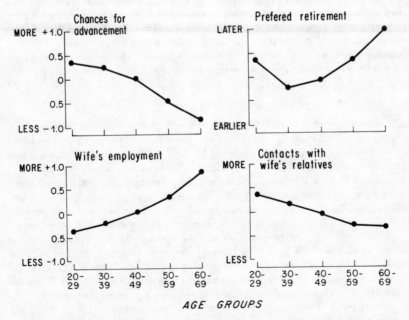

Figure 1. Four selected components of social age (change in mean values, in standardized units, over 10-year age groups).

about remaining in the saddle than those who have been working longer; while those who have been working still longer revert back to later preferred retirement. It is the middle group, then, that prefers early retirement, not those entering the occupational role or those closer to the socially expected termination of the occupational role.

Secular Effect

One must also consider a secular effect in the data, in accordance with which older subjects would be less apt to be subject to mandatory retirement schemes, due to the expansion of mandatory retirement over time within the occupational structure. Fortunately, a secular effect is not likely in this population, since under a secular effect, older subjects would have a lower education and occupational level which in turn are related to lower age of occupational retirement. In this particular population, however, education and occupational level are not related to age (r = .02), although higher education and Warner occupational level are related to later age of expected retirement (r = .18 and .12 respectively). Under these circumstances, it may be inferred that the relationship between expected age of retirement and chronological age is secular free.

Criteria of Relative Importance

Table 3 presents the differences in relative importance of the variables depending on the criterion used to judge relative importance. The increase in variance accounted for in the dependent variable by each variable stepped in is a measure of the importance of each respective variable. This amount of variance, however, may be influenced by the order in which the variable is stepped in. The use of betz x r neutralizes this effect. For the two highest and two lowest ranking variables, there is little difference no matter what criterion of relative importance is used. However, for the middle variables (variables 4 to 6 in Table 2) the rank based on R^2 change is higher than is achieved through use of beta x r. The two variables (variables 7 and 8) which maximally show the opposite effect are among the less important variables. Beta and F correspond fairly well.

Interaction Effects

Table 4 gives a picture of interaction effects among the independent variables resulting from their intercorrelations. These effects are shown from the stepwise changes in the relative importance of variables as indexed by the F value. Table 5 selectively shows initial F, selection F and final F of each variable in the equation. Initial F in Table 4 is in the column under step 1; selection F is located just above the diagonal line in Table 4 and final F is in the column under step 10 in Table 4.

Tables 6 and 7 respectively show two opposite types of interaction effects, decrease in F of V_1 when a subsequent variable V_2 is entered, and increase in F of V_1 with a subsequent entry. The first occurs if V_1 and V_2 share a common variance with the criterion. Thus, when the V_2 is entered, they share the common variance with the criterion, and the F between V_1 and the criterion goes down. In the second case, the entry of V_2 does not involve sharing of a common variance with the criterion. Thus, the variance V_2 as an unmeasured variable shared with V_1 suppresses the variance of V_1 with the criterion. Upon entry of V_2 into the measurement set, however, the suppressant effect lifts and the variance between V_1 and the criterion accordingly increases.

TABLE 6

Decrease in F of Previously Selected Variables
Shown from Evolution of F Values in Stepwise Regression*

Previously Selected Variable (V_1)	Preferred Retirement	Preferred Retirement	Contacts with Wife's Family
Step at which V_1 Selected	2	2	5
Newly Selected Variable (V_2)	Expected Retirement	Rank in Company	Contacts S's Family
Step at which V_2 Selected	8	4	9
Decrease in F of V_1			
from:	55.3	71.4	34.6
to:	18.8	54.5	18.1
	(at step 8)	(at step 4)	(at step 9)
$R_{V_1 V_2}$	.55	.18	.39
Decrease in F of V_2 when V_1 Selected			
from:	46.3	46.2	26.0
to:	9.7	31.6	10.3
	(at step 2)	(at step 2)	(at step 5)

*Data selected from Table 4

TABLE 7

Increase in F of Previously Selected Variables
Shown from Evolution of F Values in Stepwise Regression*

Previously Selected Variable (V_1)	Chances for Advancement	Chances for Advancement	Preferred Retirement
Step at which V_1 Selected	1	1	2
Newly Selected Variable (V_2)	Remain in Company	Rank in Company	Remain in Company
Step at which V_2 Selected	3	4	3
Increase in F of V_1			
from:	76.4	88.3	60.8
to:	88.3	110.8	71.4
	(at step 3)	(at step 4)	(at step 3)
$R_{V_1 V_2}$	.05	.17	-.05
Increase in F of V_2 when V_1 selected			
from:	—	—	48.7
to:			59.1
			(at step 2)

*Data selected from Table 4.

Decrease in F. In Table 4 preferred retirement decreased in Step 4 when rank in company was introduced and in step 8 when expected retirement was introduced. In each case, preferred retirement was significantly correlated with the introduced variable. Also, in the first case where the correlation between preferred retirement and expected retirement was very high, .55, the drop in F was greater than in the second case, when the r between preferred retirement and rank in company was lower, .18. In any case, the related variables shared in the accounting of variance in chronological age, an effect which appeared when they were both introduced into the equation.

Because preferred retirement shares variance with expected retirement and rank in company, preferred retirement experienced a reduction in F when these 2 latter variables were introduced. Conceptually, the linkage between preferred and expected retirement is clear. If an individual prefers to retire later, he would naturally choose a later retirement option with his retirement scheme. The special linkage between preferred retirement and rank in company may be interpreted as a special causal relationship between higher rank and preference for later retirement.

The third illustration of drop in F as shown in Table 6, is the decrease in F of contacts with wife's family when the highly related variable, contact with S's family, is introduced. The 2 variables in this case are highly related both conceptually and statistically, just as are the variables, preferred retirement and expected retirement. The distributions of these family variables show a matrilateral effect with more contact with wife's relatives than husband's relatives. The special linkage from the change in F values suggests that a decrease in the dominant matrilateral effect occasions a decrease in the patrilateral relationship. Since the subject tends to be older than his wife, her relatives are more apt to survive his relatives as the conjugal pair grows older. Therefore, contacts with subject's relatives on this basis should drop off more with age. In the regression equation, however, lessened contacts with wife's family is a more important predictor of age, so that some basic factor must be operating, such as greater importance of matrilateral influence to begin with. In this view, there would be greater matrilateral reduction with age since there is more matrilaterality to begin with.

For each of the 3 cases, Table 6 also refers to drop in F value of the unentered variable when the variable to which it is linked enters the equation. This is the obverse of the effect already discussed. When both variables were unentered, they shared a common variance and when separated due to entry on one of them, the entered variable takes some of this away, with the result that the unentered variable drops in F. This effect simply corroborates the linkages already discussed.

In the case of preferred retirement, the sharing of variance with a highly related variable caused the final F value to fall below a substantial number of other variables which had been selected later. These were: remain in company, rank in company, contacts with wife's family, relocation plans and wife's employment. Actually this happened immediately at step 8 when expected retirement entered, and held up through step 10. The same effect caused moving plans and wife's employment to move ahead of contacts with wife's family when contacts with subject's family was entered.

The moral is that redundancy in independent variables which are significantly related to the dependent variable reduces the importance of each of the redundant variables. It may not always be wise, however, to allow only non-redundant variables to enter the initial independent variable set, since redundancies are always partial and redundant variables may be conceptually distinct, as they are in this case. It would be better, then, to keep in mind the effect of redundancy as a constraint in interpreting the results.

Increase in F. Table 7 shows the opposite effect of *increase* in F of a previously entered variable when a new variable is entered. Here, chances for advancement become more important in step 3 when the suppressor variable, remain in company, is entered, and even more important in step 4 when another suppressor variable, rank in company, is introduced. In addition, introduction of remain in company in step 3 has a potentiating effect on preferred retirement. Here also a higher r between V_1 and V_2 is related to a larger change in the F, as shown by the couplet, rank in company and chances for advancement. An accompanying increase in F occurs in the unentered variable, remain in company, when preferred retirement is entered in step 2. This effect does not apply to the unentered variables, remain in company and rank in company, in connection with entry of chances for advancement, since chances for advancement entered at step 1.

The effects of the two variables, expecting to remain with the company longer and self-rating regarding higher rank in company, make reduced chances for advancement a *more* powerful predictor of age. It will be recalled from Table 6 that higher rank in company makes later preferred retirement a *less* powerful predictor of age. On the other hand, remaining longer with company makes later preferred retirement a *more* powerful predictor of age.

Relationship to other Functional Ages

In addition to social age, a biochemistry age, a personality age (from 16 PF) and an abilities age (from GATB) were derived by the multiple regression technique. The most important variables ($F < 1.0$) from each sector of functional age were then placed in a regression, from which emerged an overall functional age. In this overall measure, social variables accounted for 28 percent of the accountable variance, the clinical measures accounted for 20 percent, personality measures accounted for 4 percent, and the ability measures accounted for 48 percent. The latter was mainly an effect of the Disassemble test of the GATB, which appears to be of a far different order of magnitude than any of the other variables used. The details of the other domains of functional age and of overall functional age will be set forth in other papers.

The above represents an initial step in the development of social age with data of the Normative Aging Study. Further steps will be taken as previously outlined. It is hoped that this method of organizing the data will shed light on the social factors involved in aging, and more important, will portray the contextual role of other factors involved as part of the total aging process.

NOTES

1. This paper is from the Normative Aging Study, Benjamin Bell M.D., Director, VA Outpatient Clinic, 17 Court St., Boston, Mass. 02108. Computations were supported by funds from the Council for Tobacco Research-U.S.A.

REFERENCES

Bell, B., Rose, C. L., and Damon, A. The Veterans Administration longitudinal study of healthy aging. *The Gerontologist,* 1966, *4,* 179-184.

Benge, E. V., and Copell, D. F. Employee morale survey. *Modern Management,* 1947, *7,* 19-22.

Birren, J. E. Principles of research on aging. In J. E. Birren, ed. *Handbook of aging and the individual.* Chicago: University of Chicago Press, 1959. Pp. 18-20.

Bureau of Employment Security, U.S. Dept. of Labor, *Manual for the General Aptitude Test Battery, Section III. Development.* U.S. Govt. Printing Office, Washington, D.C., 1967.

Cattell, R. B., Eber, H. W., and Tatsuoka, M. M. *Handbook for the Sixteen Personality Factor Questionnaire (16 PF).* Institute for Personality & Ability Testing. Champaign, Ill., 1957.

Heron, A., and Chown, S. *Age and function.* Boston: Little, Brown, 1967.

Hoffman, P. J. Assessment of the independent contributions of predictors. *Psychol. Bull.*, 1962, *59*, 77-89.

Lenski, G. E. Status crystallization: a non-vertical dimension of social status. *Am. Sociol. Rev.*, 1954, *19*, 405-413.

Rose, C. L., and Bell, B. *Predicting longevity: methodology and critique.* Lexington, Mass.: D.C. Heath & Co., 1971.

chapter 6

"THE AGES OF ME": TOWARD PERSONAL AND INTERPERSONAL DEFINITIONS OF FUNCTIONAL AGING[1]

Robert Kastenbaum, Valerie Derbin, Paul Sabatini and Steven Artt

How should a person's age be established or judged? One popular answer is that a person is "as old as he feels." Perhaps an even more popular rejoinder is that a person is *"only* as old as he feels." While the personal definition is unlikely to replace all other approaches, it does appear reasonable to include self-report as a legitimate and potentially useful entry. In this paper we report on the early stages of an attempt to define and assess age from the personal frame of reference. The study also includes a quest for an interpersonal definition of age and an exploration of the relationships between personal and interpersonal frames.

BACKGROUND

Three strands of interest have been interwoven into the present research sequence:

(1) The attempt to *induce* and *modify* behavior syndromes characteristic of the aged;
(2) The attempt to expand and refine the concept of *functional age;* and
(3) Curiosity about the way in which gerontologists view their own development and aging.

Induction and Modification of "Old" Behavior

Gerontologic research has been more descriptive than experimental. The imbalance is most extreme in the social and behavioral branches. We have not mounted a systematic

71

effort to induce, modify or reverse the behavioral syndrome that is taken to be characteristic of "old age." How has it happened that the classic experimental approach, so crucial to the advancement of other scientific disciplines, has not been pursued here? We do not know the answer to this question. It is likely, however, that the following factors have influenced our disinclination to experiment:

(1) Descriptive knowledge is valuable and perhaps deserves priority in so new a field of inquiry.
(2) There are neither suitable concepts nor techniques available for the experimental induction and modification of aging in the psychosocial sphere.
(3) It goes against our grain to contemplate a program of deliberately inducing or simulating aging: should we not bend our efforts to prevent old age or bring back youth?
(4) Moral and ethical problems arise when we even begin to consider the possibility of inducing "old age."
(5) There is no guarantee that a vigorous experimental program would actually result in the induction of "old" behaviors, or their modification/reversal even if induced.

We do not wish to convey the impression that the feasibility and desirability of an experimental program has been thoroughly evaluated and subsequently set aside. The fact is that the issue has seldom been aired even as a possibility.

One cannot easily dismiss the (guessed-at) inhibiting factors mentioned above. In our opinion, however, these points do not compel indefinite paralysis. We will never know if the conceptual, methodological, temperamental and ethical problems can be solved unless the challenge is taken up. It would seem a pity to lose by forfeit!

Previous articles and reports have introduced theoretical, procedural, and empirical material relevant to the experimental induction or simulation of "old" behavior (Kastenbaum 1968, 1969a, 1969b, 1971). This material will not be repeated here. Essentially, our strategy has been to attempt to induce a syndrome of "old" behavior in adults who are not aged—but to do so by psychosocial means only, and in miniaturized forms that would produce transitory, self-limiting effects. Pastalan has recently reported an independently conceived project in which young adults moved through their daily activities under the handicap of age-simulating sensory impairments (1971). Neither Pastalan's work nor ours has "proven" anything yet, but the preliminary experiences have been on the moderately encouraging side.

There are many ways one might go about attempting to induce "old" behavior. There are even more ways in which each attempt could fail. To anchor our experimental efforts more securely we decided to pursue the following research sequence:

(1) Develop means of differentiating among people who have distinctly different views of their age status although all sharing the same chronological age. The rough categories would be "younger than my age"; "older than my age"; and "neither younger nor older than my age."
(2) Determine the relationship between subjective or personal age and objective measures of functioning. Do people who "feel" younger, for example, also "test" younger?
(3) Explore biographical-developmental factors associated with being a person who is "younger" or "older" than his chronological age.

(4) Determine the relative susceptibility of "youngers" and "olders" to an experimental program of inducing "old" behaviors, and study the strategies they employ to cope with the experimental situations.

At present we are completing a study intended to achieve some of the objectives stated in the first point above. This study has also been designed to explore functional aging from the personal and interpersonal frames of reference.

Functional Age

Physicians are well acquainted with the fact that people may have "young arteries" or "old kidneys" in relation to the norms of bodily functioning expected at certain chronological age levels. Many employers appreciate the fact that work output declines markedly for some fifty-or sixty-year-olds while others at the same age show no decline at all. It appears both reasonable and useful to augment (or challenge) chronological age with functional criteria in all spheres: biological, psychological, and social. The emergence of functional aging as a powerful concept obviously would influence theory and research in gerontology. Many political, economic and personal repercussions might also follow if the concept gains more general acceptance. Clearly, then, the concept of functional aging and its supporting evidence must be cultivated with both diligence and caution.

Heron and Chown helped to energize research in this area with their little book on *Age and Function* (Heron and Chown, 1967). Perhaps the most extensive ongoing research effort is the one that has been undertaken by a multidisciplinary team at the Boston Veterans Administration Out-Patient Clinic. Methodology and early findings are reported elsewhere in this issue. Particularly relevant to the present study are the explorations of psychological (Fozard, 1972), social (Rose, 1972), and anthropological age (Damon, 1972). While the VA Normative Aging Study has concentrated upon external and objective assessments of functional age, we have delved into the subjective frame.

Viewed as a contribution to functional aging, the present study is an attempt to develop instruments, concepts, and preliminary data that would lead to recognition of personal and interpersonal age as useful components of total functional aging.

Subjective Age Perceptions of Gerontologists

Other people may permit their preconceptions, insecurities and needs to influence their observations of aging and the aged. The gerontologist is the exception. His own relationship to the aging process is neutral, objective, normal, under control. Perceptions of his own age do not enter into his work as sources of potential error.

The proposition stated above may be true. But it has not been proven true—indeed, it has never been put to the test. We know very little, in systematic fashion, about the personal characteristics of those who study aging. Lacking data to the contrary, it may be most prudent to forego assumptions about the possible uniqueness of gerontologists as "neutral" or "objective" scientists. Donahue has called attention to a possible bias factor in the age match-up between researcher and subject (Donahue, 1965). On a broader front, it might be worth pondering the relationship between a gerontologist's total relationship to his own aging process and his scientific/professional activities. At present we do not know whether people who are attracted to gerontology are either more or less concerned about problems of personal aging than people in general. We also do not know enough about the future gerontologist's personal orientation to select appropriate learning experiences for him or capitalize upon his special strengths and sensitivities.

We decided to indulge our curiosity in this area by including a sample of gerontologists-in-training in the present study.

TERMINOLOGY

Confusion is an ever present danger once we step beyond the familiar guideline of chronological age. The definitions that follow are intended only to tag and differentiate those concepts that are most basic to the present study. More appropriate terminology can be formulated as our knowledge increases. Each of the terms proposed below is considered to be a component or dimension of the broader concept of functional age.

By *personal age* we mean the individual's self-report of his age status: how old he seems to himself. By *interpersonal age* we mean the age status of an individual as evaluated by others.

Each of these terms can be further differentiated as appears useful. We could speak either of personal age or personal age*s*. The plural form opens the possibility that even within the subjective realm there might be multiple dimensions along which age should be assessed. It also opens the possibility that the number and types of subjective dimensions might be related systematically to the individual's developmental level. Interpersonal age also could be treated either as a unitary measure or as a confederation of specific ages (e.g., "She looks like such a young thing, but she is wise beyond her years"). Additionally, interpersonal age could be constructed from the perspective of one or of several observers. Both personal and interpersonal age could be evaluated either on a one-time, situational basis or over a more extended period of time (characteristic or baseline age).

The relationship between personal and interpersonal age might be expressed in terms of *consensual age*. Close agreement between self-perception and perception-by-others would constitute a firm consensual age. Two components are involved in establishment of consensual age: a measure of inter-rater agreement, and the actual age or age-direction for which agreement has been found. It should be made clear that neither interpersonal nor consensual age is concerned primarily with the ability of others to guess the individual's chronological age. The ratings often will involve estimates of chronological age. The point, however, is to establish the degree of consensuality concerning the personal component of functional age. The observer might know for a fact that he is observing a man who is thirty years of age. If he believes this man looks ten years older, and the man himself believes he looks ten years younger, than we have an instance in which no consensual age can be established.

Personal and interpersonal age are each established on the basis of direct reports, e.g.: "I have the interests of a man of 50," or "He has the interests of a man of 35." By contrast, consensual age is determined by logico-statistical operations performed on two or more sets of observations, e.g., the two statements quoted above.

The terms that have been introduced here should be distinguished from other functional age constructs whose verbal labels are somewhat similar. (Eventually, perhaps, it will be possible to formulate a standard table of functional ages in which agreed-upon symbols take the place of ambiguous, vague-edged terminology.) Perhaps the most similar-sounding concept to those introduced here is that of *social age.* Rose has defined social age "as the predicted age yielded by a multiple regression equation composed of weighted social variables and a constant. Individuals whose social life styles are the same as those of their age peers would have a social age the same as their chronological age" (Rose, 1972). Social age differs from personal and interpersonal ages in the following ways: (a) social age is the outcome of statistical manipulations of multifaceted data, while personal and interpersonal age essentially come from one source each and are more direct "sources" or "ratings"; (b) social age is constructed from a mix of both objective and subjective data, while personal and interpersonal age rely entirely upon subjective appraisal, whether by self or other; (c) social age is based upon a set of pre-specified criteria, while appraisal of personal and interpersonal age require (or allow) the perceiver to exercise his own judgment as to what constitutes salient and admissible evidence; (d) personal and interpersonal ages are devised to serve as checks upon each other (consensual age) and thus contribute to our understanding of human interaction dynamics, while social age provides a sort of affiliation index between the individual and his chronological age cohort. Perhaps the distinction can be put another way: social age could be read as "sociol-ogical age," and personal/interpersonal age could be read as "phenomenological" and "intersubjective" age.

It is unfortunate that terminology is such a burden at this stage in functional age research, but one must run the risk of seeming overly-pedantic at times—or take the consequences of tenuous connections among concepts, methods, and findings.

STATEMENT OF PROBLEM

The basic aim of this study is to uncover the problems that must be worked through before the concepts of personal, interpersonal and consensual age can be introduced fruitfully into the general domain of functional age. Broadly stated, the major questions are:

(1) Is personal age adequately represented as a unitary construct?
(2) What is the general relationship between personal and chronological age?
(3) Is interpersonal age adequately represented as a unitary construct?
(4) Is consensual age generally capable of being established, or must personal and interpersonal age generally be treated as two very distinct constructs?

There are many other specific questions and hypotheses involved, but the above are basic in the sense that future research pathways will be strongly influenced by the way in which these questions are answered. As the study is still in progress, we will be able to report upon only a few aspects of the total range of data being obtained.

PROCEDURE

A. Instruments

1. "The Ages of Me"

A structured interview format was developed to study personal age. The basic procedure is administration of a 49-item interview schedule which has been designated, "The Ages of Me." It is given on an individual basis for purposes of this study, but can also be administered to groups. (The individual interview format, although more effortful and time-consuming, was preferred for this first study because of its potential for teaching us more about both the subject-matter and the directions in which the instrument might be usefully modified.)

Participants are told:

"Most people have other 'ages' besides their official or chronological age. We may feel or look younger or older than our chronological age. The questions we are asking you here all have something to do (directly or indirectly) with the various possible ages of you.

"This is an early phase of the study. We are just learning how to ask the right questions. By 'right questions' we mean questions that are clear and to the point. In some instances you will notice that we are asking essentially the same question in two different ways. This is being done to help us decide which form of the question is most useful.

"We appreciate your cooperation in this study. Any comments or suggestions you would care to offer about these questions would be most welcome."

The first set of items requests comparative ratings. There are five fixed-alternative questions:

Most of the time I *feel*
Most of the time I *look*
My *interests* and *activities* are most like those of
People who know me *casually* regard me as
People who know me *very well* regard me as.

The following response choices are provided:

Quite a bit older than most people my age
A little older than most people my age
Neither older nor younger than most people my age
A little younger than most people my age
Quite a bit younger than most people my age.

(The wording is slightly different for the *interests* and *activities* question, e.g., "People who are quite a bit older than myself.")

This set of items also includes three open-end questions, requesting the S to specify the interests and activities he had in mind, and to indicate the probable basis upon which other people judge his relative age.

The second set of items includes four questions that request specification of an absolute age instead of a comparison:

I *feel* as though I were about age:
I *look* as though I were about age:
I *do* most things as though I were about age:
My *interests* are mostly those of a person about age:

There are also two open-end items in this set:

If there is anything about me that is "young for my age," it is probably:
If there is anything about me that is "old for my age," it is probably:

The third set consists of nine items dealing with the S's past. These questions are included to obtain clues for more systematic study into antecedent conditions of those who classify themselves as younger or older than their current chronological age (e.g., "When I was a child, my parents tended to treat me as though I were: quite a bit more grown up than most other children my age . . . a little more grown up . . . neither more nor less grown up . . . a little less grown up . . . quite a bit less grown up than most other children my age.").

The fourth set is concerned with S's comfort with his age and also his sense of comfort with people of various ages. The items alternate between fixed-alternative and open-end responses. Among the items most relevant to the present report are:

(No. 25) If I could pick out the age I would like to be right now, I would select age:

(No. 26) Why? Please explain your answer

(No. 27) At this time in my life I am (five fixed-alternatives from "entirely comfortable with my present age" to "very uncomfortable with my present age").

(No. 28) The reason I gave this answer:

(No. 29) I would like to stay at my present age, if this were possible (five fixed-alternatives from "as long as possible" to "prefer to move to the next age a lot sooner").

The fifth set is comprised of open-end questions inquiring into the criteria S uses to appraise a person's functional age. An example is (No. 43): I can imagine two people who are each 50 years of age. One of these people seems "old" to me, the other does not. The important differences between these people are:

The sixth set consists of three more self-classification items:

If I had to classify myself according to age, I would choose to describe myself as a: (examples: teenager, adolescent, young adult, middle-aged, elder, old, aged, etc. If you have a better term to describe your own age, please use it).

I feel as though my rate of change (growing up or growing older) is now (speeding up/continuing at its previous rate/slowing down).

In general, my body is (five fixed-alternatives from "very young for my age" to "very old for my age").

Some of the Ages of Me items contribute directly to personal age scores, while others of the items provide a context for interpretation and hypothesis-generation.

2. Age-Appropriate Attitudes Technique

The research interview also includes administration of the Age-Appropriate Attitude Technique (AAAT). This procedure consists of a gallery of six fictitious people who each have a distinct outlook on life. The original form (Kastenbaum, 1963, 1964) employed masculine names only; for this study, female names were employed when administered to female Ss.

The AAAT characters are presented in Table 1. The outlook listed for each character is given here to clarify the items' intent, but is not presented to the Ss.

S is asked several questions about each AAAT character:

"About what age would you say_____is? Why did you choose this age for _____? Now that you know how_____feels, what would you say to him by way of a reply? Using a five-point scale, would you strongly agree, agree, agree somewhat, disagree, or strongly disagree with this view?"

Additionally, when S has responded to all the characters individually, he is asked to indicate which of them holds a view that is most similar to his own outlook at the present time. (By comparing his choice with the dialogue he previously invented between himself and the character, we are provided with a possible insight into S's inner relationship to his own age.)

The AAAT data do not contribute directly to the personal age determination, but do provide helpful contextual information.

TABLE 1

Age-Appropriate Attitudes Technique

Character	Sketch	Outlook
Harry/Carol:	is feeling very blue. He has decided that the future holds nothing for him.	The Null Future
Phil/Ann:	wonders if he is really getting any place. He does not know whether he should be hopeful or pessimistic about his future.	The Uncertain Future
Charlie/Susie:	is feeling great. He feels that his life is just beginning, that nothing can stop him.	The Exuberant Future
Grant/Christine:	feels that he has everything he wants. He is completely satisfied with his life, and desires nothing more.	The Satiated Present
Ted/Pamela:	does not like new things. He prefers the old way of doing things, feeling that things are not as good as they used to be.	The Beloved Past
Sam/Gwen:	has no use for the old way of doing things. He prefers everything new, believing that things are getting to be much better than they used to be.	The Despised Past

3. Time Perspective Questionnaire

A brief time perspective questionnaire (Teahan and Kastenbaum, 1970) is also administered. The questionnaire inquires into past and future outlook, including specification of age-range of "happiest years," assessment of role in the future (agent vs. recipient), and both expected and desired length of lifespan.

4. Observer Rating Forms

The most relevant questions asked of the S himself are also asked of the interviewer. At the conclusion of the interview, the S's "looks," "interests," etc. are rated by the interviewer. S is also asked to provide the name of somebody who knows him well. This person is then contacted to make a parallel rating of interpersonal age (with the S's knowledge and permission).

Copies of all data-gathering procedures used in this study are available upon request from the authors.

B. Subjects

Two subpopulations are being studied at present. Students supported for advanced studies by the Institute of Gerontology (University of Michigan/Wayne State University) comprise one sample. The gerontology specialists include 27 women and 16 men with an age range from 20 to 60 years. While the number of women and men is almost equal in the 40-and-under range (16 women; 14 men), only two male students over the age of 40 could be located as compared with eleven women. The other sample is comprised of men and women who are roughly matched with the gerontologists in that they also are pursuing studies and careers involving many personal interactions, but who do not manifest any special interest in or commitment to gerontology. Most of these Ss are recruited from employees of a state agency. The nongerontologic or general sample includes 10 women and 21 men at present. The age range is comparable, with the exception of three women in the 60-65 age bracket. The total N available for analysis at this time is 75:38 women, 37 men.

RESULTS

The response of the Ss to the age-focused interview deserves brief comment. Typically, the S begins with a matter-of-fact, slightly aloof orientation. The interview is something S is prepared to "handle" in professional rather than personal terms, not surprising in view of the background of most Ss. Before long, however, the S tends to be deeply immersed. The questions seem to strike home. Some Ss make use of the interview to launch a probing self-examination of their developmental history and prospects; few seem to remain unaffected by the experience. In future studies an attempt will be made to objectify type and intensity of S's involvement in the interview per se. The gerontology specialists do not appear to be immune to the challenges of age-oriented inquiry. Several gerontologists are among those who expressed the greatest amount of perturbation during and after the interview. (This reaction tends to confirm earlier impressions by the authors that gerontology training programs do not invariably prepare specialists to cope with age-related problems on a personal basis.)

1. Personal Age

Ss are asked to rate their own age status in two ways: by comparing themselves with others at the same chronological age (Item Set 1), and by specifying the absolute chronological age that most closely matches the way they look, feel, think, and act (Item Set 2). This analysis will be limited to the absolute age mode of response which, on available evidence, appears to be a more sensitive index. The following illustrative data bear on the questions of unitary vs. multidimensional structure of personal age, and the relationship between personal and chronological age at various levels of chronological age.

One obvious question concerns the general level of agreement between personal and chronological age. The percentage of Ss who gave their actual chronological age in response to each of the four personal age questions being considered here was computed. This provides percentage-of-agreement data on "feel age," "look age," "do age," and "interests age" for five chronological age categories: 20's, 30's, 40's, 50's, and 60's (the latter with such a small N at present that no conclusions are warranted).

Inspection of the results indicates that agreement between personal and chronological age occurs only to a moderate extent. Of the 20 figures displayed in Table 2, only one shows as much as a 50 percent agreement (interest age at chronological age 30). The range of agreement percentages scales all the way down to 0 percent (look age at chronological age 50). The lack of comparative data from other populations severely limits our ability to specify how "high" or "low" these consistency percentages might be. It is clear, however, that knowledge of a person's chronological age cannot be substituted for direct knowledge of his age status in his own eyes. Personal age, in other words, does appear to be a concept distinct enough from chronological age that they cannot be interchanged without the likelihood of gross error.

Next, one can turn to the same set of data for information concerning age trends. The mean percentage of agreement between personal and chronological ages declines steadily throughout the adult decades (but one must not lose sight of the fact that these

TABLE 2

Percentage of Ss Expressing Agreement Between
Chronological and Personal Age

Decade	Look Age	Feel Age	Do Age	Interests Age	Mean %
20's	44%	41%	41%	38%	41%
30's	20%	30%	40%	50%	35%
40's	35%	30%	20%	20%	26%
50's	0%	20%	20%	10%	12.5%
60's	33%	33%	16%	16%	−

data are cross-sectional). While men and women in their 20's express 41 percent agreement (across specific personal age items), this figure dips to 12.5 percent for those in their 50's. The decline in agreement decade by decade shows a 6 percent drop between 20's and 30's, another 9 percent for the 40's, and 13.5 percent for the 50's. The declines for the 40's and 50's are especially striking when it is understood each is subtracted from a progressively lower agreement figure for the preceding (younger) decade. (Data on the 60's are indicated for sake of completeness, but will not be included in further analysis and interpretation until a more ample N has been obtained.)

This pattern suggests what might be characterized as an increasing personalization of personal age with advancing chronological age. If we wished to arrive at a general expression of agreement between chronological and personal age, then we would have to qualify the usefulness of this term very heavily, or incorporate an age-correction term. The mean percentage of agreement for the present sample turns out to be 32.7 percent (computed on the basis of the actual N for each decade, rather than taking the mean from the percentages given for unequal N's in Table 2). While this figure happens to come close to the consistency shown by 30 year-olds between their personal and chronological ages, it would prove more misleading than helpful in evaluating the general relationship between personal and chronological age. Unless subsequent data reverse the present trend, it will be necessary to recognize a widening disparity between personal and chronological age throughout the adult years.

Of equal interest to percentage of agreement is the question of directionality. Do people tend to regard themselves as younger or older than their chronological ages, or can any generalization be made? On the basis of the limited data currently available, this problem can be addressed directly: (a) personal age tends to be younger than chronological age, and (b) the bias toward a younger personal age is found in an increasingly conspicuous form as we move upward in the chronological age scale. In other words, most of the increasing gap between chronological and personal age already noted can be accounted for in terms of a bias toward self-reported youthfulness.

One of the ways in which the directional trend can be expressed is in terms of algebraic mean for inconsistencies between personal and chronological age. A deviation toward older personal age arbitrarily was recorded as positive, and deviation toward younger personal age recorded as negative. Equal inconsistencies in both directions would result in an algebraic mean of zero. As can be seen in Table 3, all of the 20 item-by-decade computations show a bias toward personal age being reported as younger than chronological age. The bias begins in a modest way with the 20 year-olds whose algebraic means favored youthful self-evaluations by differentials such as -.66

TABLE 3

Direction and Extent of Inconsistencies Between
Chronological and Personal Ages*

Decade	Look Age	Feel Age	Do Age	Interests Age
20's	-.66	-.72	-.69	-.83
30's	-.80	-2.90	-4.30	-1.20
40's	-2.85	-6.30	-6.40	-7.80
50's	-7.60	-8.30	-12.60	-13.20
60's	-4.66	-9.33	-16.60	-15.50

*Negative sign=personal age younger than chronological. Positive sign would=personal age older than chronological, but no such instances were found.

(look age) and -.72 (feel age). By the time we reach the 50-year-olds, however, all discrepancies between personal and chronological age are in the youthful direction, with means ranging from -7.6 (look age) up to -13.2 (interests age).

The data already presented have implications for the dimensional structure of personal age. The age a person believes that he looks tends to be that aspect of personal age which is closest to chronological age. In Table 3, for example, look age shows the smallest youthward bias for every decade represented, while interests age shows the greatest youthward bias. The gap between look and interests also appears to widen with every decade (from a -.17 differential in the 20's to a -5.80 in the 50's). Given this trend toward systematic difference among personal age dimensions, it might be premature to treat personal age as a unitary variable at this time.

It is perhaps even more relevant, however, to examine directly the internal consistency of personal age responses apart from their relationship to chronological age. Simple inspection of the data revealed that only 13 of the 75 Ss specified the same personal age for each of the four items—in other words, about 80 percent of the sample expressed some internal inconsistency. (Inconsistency is not intended to be a negative value term here; it also could be said that people who give more than one age have a more highly differentiated view of their personal age.) Incidentally, four of the 13 consistent individuals specified a personal age that was different from their chronological age. At the opposite extreme, there were 11 Ss who gave a different age for every item. Another 25 Ss specified three different ages for the four personal age items. In other words, almost half of the sample (36/75) showed a high degree of internal variation on the personal age items. Another interesting group was the set of 19 Ss who gave three identical ages, but one that was different. It turned out that look age was clearly the most often "out-grouped" dimension: nine Ss were internally consistent for the other three items, with the remaining ten Ss distributed randomly in their choice of an item to break the consistency pattern.

Further information can be obtained by counting the number of instances in which a particular personal age item received the same response as another item. Percentage of consistency among the four personal age items is shown in Table 4. One of the most striking results is the low ceiling for inter-item agreement. No pair of items was given the same age more than 50 percent of the time. How old a person feels was in agreement 49 percent of the time with the response to "I do most things as though I were about age . . . " The lowest agreement also involved do age: this item showed only 28 percent consistency with feel age.

Overall, when Ss specified their look age, they were giving a response that had only a

TABLE 4

Consistency Percentage Among Personal Age Items

	Look Age	Feel Age	Do Age	Interests Age	Mean %
Look Age		45.33%	28.00%	33.33%	35.55%
Feel Age	45.33%		49.33%	44.33%	46.22%
Do Age	28.00%	49.33%		45.33%	40.89%
Interests Age	33.33%	44.33%	45.33%		40.89%

35.55 percent mean consistency with their other personal age items. How old they *feel*, however, provides the best clue to general personal age with a consistency percentage of 46 percent. *Do* and *interests* age fell almost exactly halfway between *look* and *feel*.

It is interesting to see that while a person's evaluation of his *look* age is closest to chronological age, it is his *feel* age that most nearly approaches an index to his broader view of personal age.

2. Interpersonal and Consensual Ages

There are two sources of interpersonal age data in this study: interviewer ratings and ratings made by an acquaintance of *S*. We will consider here only the ratings made by the interviewer on two items: how old the *S looks* to him, and how old he thinks of *S* as being in *general*. About two-thirds of the time, the interviewer was consistent in his own ratings of *look* and *general* for the same *S*. As can be seen in Table 5, consistency was relatively high for the 30's and 50's (80 percent agreement), and relatively low for the 20's and 40's. Consistency of interviewer's ratings exceeds the average internal consistency of *S*'s self-ratings (Table 4). The mean *interpersonal* age consistency (65 percent) is well above any of the agreement percentages found between pairs of *personal* age items. Within the limits of these data, it would appear that the interviewer is more apt to take *look* age as an index of *general* age than is *S* himself.

TABLE 5

Interpersonal Age Consistency by Decades

Decade	Look/General Age
20's	62%
30's	80%
40's	55%
50's	80%
60's	67%

Mean interpersonal age consistency: 65%

Illustrative data on *consensual* age are presented in Table 6. Two *personal* age items (*look* and *feel*) are each paired with the two *interpersonal* age items (*look* and *general*) given above. Interviewer and *S* are furthest apart when we match "I *feel*" with the interviewer's rating of *general* age. Perhaps this is consistent with a finding presented above, namely, that *feel* is the component of *personal* age that is least predictable from knowledge of chronological age, a more inward dimension than *look*.

A number of age trends are suggested by the data in Table 6, but none are clear enough to seize upon at the moment. The usefulness of various items for establishing

TABLE 6

Consensual Age Consistency by Decades

Decade	Look/Look	Feel/General	Look/General	Decade Mean %
20's	72%	45%	44%	53.66%
30's	40%	40%	40%	40%
40's	55%	50%	55%	53.33%
50's	50%	50%	70%	56.66%
60's	50%	83%	100%	77.66%
mean %	56%	46.7%	55%	

consensuality seems to depend upon *S*'s chronological age. *S* and interviewer agree 70 percent of the time, for example, if *S* is in his 50's and the comparison is between personal *look* and interpersonal *general*. The same comparison, however, yields only a 44 percent consensus if the *S* is in his 20's. At some age levels (30's and 40's) consensus is virtually identical no matter what specific ratings are being compared—but marked differences are found at other age levels (20's and 50's). The consistently low agreement between *S* and interviewer for the 30's opens a problem area that will be explored in more detail in later studies and reports. People in their 30's were the only *S*s in the present study who showed any substantial trend toward seeing themselves as both younger and older than their chronological age. The youthward trend is already established for the 20's, as reported above, and accelerates from the 40's onward. While the person in his 30's tends to be a participant in the "younger-than-my-age" movement, he also has some thoughts in the opposite direction as well.

3. Contextual Data

Only a few illustrations can be given here of data emerging from the AAAT and Time Perspective Questionnaire. "Charlie/Susie," the exuberant future character of the AAAT, was easily the most popular choice as character-identified-with by the *S*s in general (38 of 75). This finding appears consistent with the youthward bias that pervades so much of the personal age data. The parallel also holds true when chronological age by decades is added to the picture. Older *S*s tended to select Charlie even more often than did the younger *S*. Charlie was the choice of 38 percent of the 20's, 50 percent of the 30's, 65 percent of the 40's, and 60 percent of the 50's (as well as by two of the six 60's). In other words, the older the *S* the more likely he is to identify with a person who believes that his life is "just beginning," and that "nothing can stop him."

Who did *not* identify with Charlie? There were no Charlies at all among *S*s who *wanted* to live much longer than they *expected* to live on the Time Perspective Questionnaire. This suggestive finding points up the importance of considering *S*'s orientation toward death along with attempting to understand his personal age. As a number of observers have remarked, it might be more useful to reckon age from date of death backward, rather than date of birth forward. Relationship between personal age and life-death expectation will be examined more intensively in future reports.

DISCUSSION

The methodological limitations of this study are numerous. As the first stage of a new research program, it is intended to replace itself as soon as possible. Apart from problems that should be readily apparent to the reader, it should be noted that the interviewers are all in the 20's age-range and are not provided with special training in estimation of interpersonal age. Both the age match-up between interviewer and S and the criteria established for interpersonal age ratings might be expected to influence the results. We did opt deliberately for the untutored rating of interpersonal age at this stage in the research. The variables of interviewer age and specificity of criteria should be explored further. It also bears repeating that our data are cross-sectional and thus do not establish anything about changes with age in the same S.

A thorough discussion is probably out of place until the N has been enlarged and the full range of data analyzed. There are a few points, however, which deserve mention here.

(1) We had not expected the bias toward a youthward personal age to show itself even in the youngest subsample. It seems traditional to assume that young people want to be "grown up" in their own and others' eyes. If so, at what age level does the switchover toward youthward self-perception begin? Is it possible that young people are less interested or less ready to see themselves as grown ups than in past generations? Or do people now feel "old enough" before their 20's, and believe that subsequent years bring little in the way of further maturation?

(2) With advancing adult age we have found an increasing tendency to express a personal age that is much discrepant from the chronological. Is it "healthy" or "pathological" to embrace an ever-more-youthful self-conception as one grows older? What are the critical differences between those who give personal ages consistent with the chronological and those who so resolutely think (themselves) young? Will, in fact, the most youthward biased Ss prove to be correspondingly youthful when tested on objective measures of functional age?

(3) As a corollary to the above, it appears somewhat unusual to find a person who considers himself "old for his age," especially in the upper age brackets. Will this trend be extended or reversed when we include people in their 70's, 80's and 90's? The strong general youthward bias, if supported in subsequent studies, would have implications for the experimental-modification line of research sketched earlier in this paper. Fairly clear-cut samples of people who consider themselves young for their age should be easy to obtain, but perhaps not so for those who classify themselves as older than their age. The entire classification system may have to be shifted to the youthward side (e.g., "much younger than my age," "somewhat younger than my age," and "not younger—but not older—than my age").

(4) The present data imply that how old a person *looks* and how old he *feels* (both from his own frame of reference) represent appreciably different aspects of his total personal age. At least these two facets should be differentiated, and perhaps others as research continues. Future efforts might be directed toward obtaining more adequate measures of *looks* and *feels* components of personal age, and to determine the relationship of each to other measures of functional age. Would the more inward dimension show a stronger relationship to subtle measures of biological age? Would the more "exposed" component of *looks* age prove more strongly related to social age?

(5) At this point, there is an impression that gerontology specialists share in the general trends that have been reported for the total sample. It is possible that this impression will be modified when all analyses have been performed. The lack of conspicuous differences, however, does suggest that involvement in specialized gerontology training (or choice of this specialty in the first place) cannot be assumed to create a cadre of adults with distinctive orientations toward their own personal age.

The possibility of including age role-playing and other self-confrontation procedures in gerontology training might be worth serious consideration.

(6) The results allow for cautious optimism concerning the possibility of establishing interpersonal and consensual age on a footing that is at least as secure as that of personal age.

CONCLUSION

Three concepts have been introduced: *personal* age (how old a person seems to himself), *interpersonal* age (how old he seems to others) and *consensual* age (degree of agreement between personal and interpersonal ages.) This initial research report, drawing from partial results on 75 adult Ss in a study still in progress, indicates that the structure of these three ages must be considered in relationship to chronological age level. The most general finding was an increased bias toward youthward evaluation (and, thus, discrepancy with chronological age) as we ascend the age ladder from the 20's through the 50's. Individuals tend to take a more differentiated view of their own age status than do interviewers. This includes a moderately clear distinction between the age a person *feels* and the age that he believes he *looks*. Interviewers had particular difficulty in assessing how old *S feels*. The overall results suggest that personal and interpersonal age can be developed into sets of concepts useful in the more general domain of functional age, and might also serve as basis for experimental attempts to create and manipulate "old" behavior. Advanced students of gerontology who participated in the study appear to share the same orientations as the population in general.

NOTES

1. This report derives from a study supported in part by The Institute of Gerontology, University of Michigan/Wayne State University.

REFERENCES

Damon, A. Predicting age from body measurements and observations. *Aging & Human Development*, 1972, 3, 169-174.

Donahue, W. Relationship of age of perceivers to their social perceptions. *Gerontologist*, 1965, 5, 241-245; 276-277.

Heron, A., and Chown, S. *Age and function*. Boston: Little, Brown & Co., 1967.

Fozard, J. L. Predicting age in the adult years from psychological assessments of abilities and personality. *Aging & Human Development*, 1972, 3, 175-182.

Kastenbaum, R. Perspectives on the development and modification of behavior in the aged: A developmental perspective. *Gerontologist*, 1968, 8, 280-284.

Kastenbaum, R. What happens to the man who is inside the aging body? An inquiry into the developmental psychology of later life. In F. C. Jeffers (ed.), *Duke University Council on Aging and Human Development. Proceedings of Seminars, 1965-1969*. Durham, North Carolina: Duke University Press, 1969a, 99-112.

Kastenbaum, R. Toward the experimental induction of "old behavior." NIMH project proposal. Detroit, Mich.: Wayne State University, 1969b.

Kastenbaum, R. Getting there ahead of time. *Psychology Today*, 1971 (December), 52-54; 82-84.

Pastalan, L. Testimony to U.S. Senate Special Committee on Aging, 1971.

Rose, C. L. The measurement of social age. *Aging & Human Development*, 1972, 3, 153-168.

chapter 7

THE EFFECT OF PERCEIVED AGE ON INITIAL IMPRESSIONS AND NORMATIVE ROLE EXPECTATIONS

Janet H. Lawrence, Ph.D.[1]

This study was an investigation of a new methodology which might be applied to measure the effect perceived age and stereotyping have on human interaction. The behavioral expectations which one associates with a person never before encountered are determined largely by initial impressions (educated guesses) about the stranger. These immediate impressions are imputed to the stranger on the basis of perceived relationships between certain audio-visual cues which the stranger displays and behaviors which the perceiver has learned to associate with these cues. Audio-visual cues may be anyone of a number of features; from physical shape or size to a tone of voice. Britton and Britton (1961) and Kastenbaum, et. al. (1971) have found that respondents were able to assess the chronological ages of other adults based on their physical characteristics. Other research indicates that chronological age is frequently associated with stereotyped behavior expectations (Tuckman and Lorge, 1953; Neugarten and Gutmann, 1958; Altrocchi and Eisdorfer, 1961; Neugarten, Moore, and Lowe, 1965; Golde, and Kogan, 1959; Kogan, 1961; Silverman, 1966; Aaronson, 1966; Traxler, 1971). Since physical age cues are constantly and immediately on display, it seems that a stranger's age may be perceived and may effect social interaction by playing a significant part in the formation of initial impressions.

Research has been conducted in the field of kinesics to evaluate the effect of a person's *facial expression* (Eckman, 1965, 1967, 1969; Birdwhistell, 1960, 1967; Teresa, 1971), various *body positions* (Fast, 1971; Goffman, 1963; Thompkins and McCarter, 1964; McDavid and Harari, 1968) and *race* (Sarbin and Allen, 1968; Secourd, Dukes, and Bevan, 1954; Secourd, 1959; Stein, Hardyck and Smith, 1965) upon initial impressions of strangers. But this writer found little investigation had been done with regard to the effect a person's physical age appearance has upon these same reactions. Most of the research in the area of age stereotyping has been directed toward the identification of beliefs and attitudes which people attribute to different age groups; not the effect those beliefs have on specific behavior.

In light of this, the study was designed so that the *extent* to which age-related beliefs and attitudes are utilized might be examined. The *existence* of stereotypes was assumed and an attempt was made to *establish a baseline for the frequency* with which age was used in relation to other cues.

To determine these baselines, two sets of TAT-type photographs were developed. One set showed people face-on in a very controlled pose and environment so that the only cues available were part of the person's appearance. The other set was designed so that in addition to their physical appearances, there was information regarding certain social roles they could be playing. Data were collected and analyzed, in the first instance, in terms of how often the person's perceived age was considered compared to other information. In the second case, data were collected to determine how important age was as a central aspect of role expectations.

LIMITATIONS OF THE STUDY

Because of the vast amount of information which may be utilized in interpersonal perception, certain experimental limits were used to reduce the scope of the problem. The most important of these limitations were as follows:

1. The study was limited to the visual cues which people may use to form initial impressions. This does not mean that other information is not used; it was simply necessary to control the amount of stimulus input so that the relative importance of various cues could be determined.

2. Only the cues which subjects utilized, not the attributes which people associated with them, were analyzed. This was done because the purpose was to examine the extent perceived age was utilized and not to examine the specific conjoint associations subjects made between cues and personality attributes.

3. The models in the photographs and the subjects were caucasians. Racial differences were controlled in order to make comparisons between age and socio-economic groups more meaningful.

METHOD

Rationale

When devising the measurement instruments used in this study, certain theoretical assumptions were made about the cognitive processes involved in initial impression formation. The first was that *people are able to form initial impressions on the basis of limited information*. Previous studies by Asch (1946), Wells, Goi and Seader (1958), and McDavid and Harari (1966), for example, demonstrated that subjects were able to formulate initial impressions under minimal information input conditions.

The second assumption was that in this study, *the initial impressions formed by the subjects would be the result of stereotyping.* Interpersonal perception may take place on at least two levels of complexity. First, there are the initial impressions which one holds before he has an opportunity to interact with a stranger. Second, there are those perceptions which one develops after he has interacted with the person and has had an opportunity to check out some of his initial thoughts. The cognitive organization and interpretation processes operating on the first level are thought to comprise stereotyping because a person tends to utilize over-generalized and simplified information categories to encode limited stimulus input and make character judgments. Stereotyping is a part of the perceptual process which consists of the "construction of a set of organized categories in terms of which stimulus inputs may be sorted, given identity, and given more elaborated connotative meaning" (Brunner, 1957). Concept formation (initial impressions) is thus analogous to a sorting and filing system in which perceptual experiences are sorted into categories which are differentially open to the assimilation of new input. Experienced objects or events that have common elements, attributes or qualities are likely to be perceptually sorted into the same category and elicit similar responses.

The third major assumption was that *there is a category into which associative relationships between chronological age and expected behavior are sorted. Furthermore, if one experimentally controls the amount of input, the extent to which perceived age is utilized may be determined.*

As mentioned before, Britton and Britton (1961) found that subjects were able to identify the chronological age of strangers based on physical features. Kastenbaum, et. al. (1971) found that interpersonal age, the age status of an individual as evaluated by others, was most often calculated on the basis of physical appearance and that looks were closely correlated with the person's chronological age. Therefore, it seems reasonable to assume people are able to calculate a stranger's chronological (interpersonal) age on the basis of his physical appearance.

The "implicit theory of personality" (Hays, 1958) has been developed to explain the cognitive process by means of which appearance cues become linked with personality traits. According to this theory, cognitive sets of inferential relationships are learned from direct or vicarious experience with people who have certain features and behave in a certain way. Since people can assess chronological age from physical features, and because they have learned to associate age with various behavioral expectations, they should use perceived age in impression formation.

Another premise upon which this study depended was that *socialization equips an individual with learned associations between certain cues and social positions and* that *cognitive sets exist in which certain role expectations are associated with these positions.* These cues thus enable the observer to form initial impressions on the basis of the perceived social role of the stranger.

Dress, environment, social distance, and age are among the various cues which people associate with certain roles. Social distance refers to the amount of space between people which society defines as appropriate for different role relationships (Trandis and Trandis, 1966). In a boss-employee situation, for example, a certain amount of space should be maintained between the two people in order for one to demonstrate respect and the other authority.

Chronological age is also thought to be associated with certain social roles. There are certain age stratification theorists who believe that age has been built into social systems as a criterion for entering or relinquishing certain roles. Riley has suggested that age takes on a normative quality since "by defining the admission of certain age strata to specified roles, other strata are excluded, having been defined as *not* possessing the requisite characteristics for role performance" (Riley, 1972; 7).

The final assumption underlying the methodology was that *chronological ages have become associated with achieved social roles in the normative manner just described.* Furthermore, the researcher thought that *the strength of this association can be calculated by manipulating the age of people in certain roles.*

Linton (1945) developed a taxonomy of roles in which he differentiated ascribed from achieved roles according to the method of allocation. Ascribed roles are those which a person assumes through no effort on his own part; those of male, female, brother, older person, etc. Achieved roles are those which a person attains by virtue of his efforts; positions with prerequisites which must be fulfilled in order for a person to perform the given role. Certain writers believe that there is an age status system in this country which has various ascribed roles associated with the positions along the age continuum. Rose (1962), Riley (1971, 1972), Linton (1945), and Cottrell (1942) have all developed theories of age stratification among which there are common elements. They believe societies are divided into age strata which form a continuum from younger to older. The cohorts in the different strata differ in the contributions they can make to the processes and activities of societies. They differ primarily in their biological and psychological maturity and based upon these differences certain activities are physiologically possible whereas others are not possible or are sanctioned.

There are opponents to the idea of this age-related role system. Burgess (1960) has written that older people are trapped in a "roleless role. They have no vital functions to perform . . . nor are they offered a ceremonial-role by society to make up in part for their lost functional role." Rosow (1967) believes that "aside from such general bromides as that old people should stay active, there is little specification of what they should do and what standards to follow." Wood (1971) believes that adulthood constitutes the major portion of the life span and that "during this long period, behavioral expectations are largely based on achieved (rather than ascribed) roles; societal expectations regarding behavior are rarely based on age alone, but rather on a combination of factors."

The truth probably lies somewhere between these extremes and one should be able to assess the strength of the associative relationship between age norms and given positions by manipulating the ages of people occupying certain roles in a given situation. In other words, it is possible that a person of a certain age, with all the expectations attributed to that age, may achieve a position with another set of expectations which might be conflicting. Thus, one should be able to assess the relative importance of role and age based expectations by manipulating the age of the person in the role.

The psychological mechanisms which should enable such an assessment to be made have been called cognitive dissonance by Festinger (1957) and transmission tuning by Zajonc (1960). The cognitive dissonance theory states that when man receives cognitions which are dissonant, he will try to make them consonant. The psychological mechanism consists of over-emphasizing one set of conflicting information either 1) to make the other seem worthwhile (as in initiation studies) or 2) to make sense out of the situation (Festinger, 1957; Aaronson and Mills, 1959).

Zajonc (1960) differentiated two sets of "readiness" to deal with information and then investigated the effects of these sets on cognitive structuring. The two sets were labelled "transmission tuning" and "reception tuning." In the first instance, the individual expects to communicate his cognitions to others; in the second, he expects to receive more information. "Zajonc's distinctions become relevant for the problems of impression-formation when we consider that the situational demands placed upon the person can be thought of as guiding the way he organizes conflicting impression material. When set to transmit his impressions to others, the person should tend to *polarize*, that is he should tend to exclude, surpress, or minimize one polarity of the contradiction and order the relevant cognitions around the other extreme" (Cohen, 1961; 199).

If there is a combination of vagueness and a potential of conflict between the age of the people in certain roles and the normative ages thought to be associated with these roles, a subject will have to resolve this conflict when he transmits his impressions. According to the theory of cognitive dissonance, if the subject perceives conflict he will need to assign roles based on the age of the people in the pictures or assign them based on some other criteria. Thus, the relative effect of age and other role associations can be assessed when the age of the actors and their roles are experimentally manipulated.

Development of the Instruments

A thematic apperception approach to the study of age stereotyping has certain advantages for studying the extent of age stereotyping. First, the responses to the stimuli are relatively uncensored. As Neugarten and Gutmann state (1958), "responses (are) relatively uncensored, more closely related to the respondent's values and experiences than those he may feel constrained to give in answer to more direct questions." Second, a TAT-type instrument provides enough structure to permit comparison of responses and yet allows freedom for uncensored and unrestrained answers. In the analysis of their TAT data, Neugarten and Gutmann (1958) found that instead of yielding complete role descriptions for each of the characters, the subjects' stories emphasized the important aspects of each role. "What was obtained was a central aspect of the role, an aspect that, in one translated form of behavior or another, is being recognized." Third, in an exploratory study the semi-structured nature of this data allows the researcher to use the inductive process to follow-up trends as they appear.

AGE APPEARANCE PHOTOGRAPHS (AAP)

This set of photographs consisted of nine people distributed as follows:

Age	Sex	Dress
Young adult	Male	Mod
	Female	Conservative
	Male	Casual
Middle-aged	Male	Mod
	Male	Conservative
	Female	Casual
Elderly	Male	Mod
	Male	Conservative
	Female	Casual

In this study, photographs were developed instead of the stick figures more common in other thematic apperception tests. First, because studies of emotional expression have found that subjects were more able to discern cues in photographs than in drawings (Frijda, 1969; Eckman, 1967, 1971; Birdwhistell, 1967). Second, because the use of photographs made the situation as life like as possible while allowing the control of information content.

Selection of models. Poloroid pictures were taken of 30 caucasians whose chronological ages fell between 25-35, 45-55, 65-75 years; those age spans taken to represent the Young Adult, Middle-age, and Elderly Experimental Age Groups. These people were selected because their physical appearance was representative of certain documented skin and postural changes which appear within these age spans.

The final models were selected from among these thirty pilot models. They were selected on the basis of evaluations made by 60 randomly selected individuals who estimated the models' chronological ages. Physiologists also evaluated the models for representative body changes. In each of the three Age Groups, the three pilot models whose ages were most often estimated were also those selected by the physiologist and they were used as the final models.

Final Pose. The final pose had two components: a) a neutral facial expression and b) experimentally manipulated dress. Eckman, Friesen, and Thompkins (1971) have developed a Facial Affect Scoring Technique (FAST) which is used to describe facial expression. For the purpose of their scale, the face is described primarily in terms of 1) tension or relaxation of specific features, 2) wrinkles, and 3) positions of features. The appearance descriptions are made separately for three facial areas: the *lower face* (consisting of cheek-nose-mouth-chin-jaw); *middle face* (eyes-lids-bridge of nose); and *upper face* (brows-forehead). A scorer may select from among six emotions or he may indicate that he thinks the facial expression is neutral. A neutral score is given "if the facial area to be scored appeared to be in a normal or rest position or the wrinkles shown were inferred to be a paramount part of the physiogomy" (Eckman, 1971).

Based on this scaling procedure, the AAP models were posed with neutral facial expressions. They were coached to relax each area of the face until the features appeared to be in rest positions. They were also posed in a neutral stance which was modeled after the classic anatomic position; standing with feet parallel, toes pointed forward, hands relaxed by the sides. The background behind the models was blank white.

One of the three models in each of the three Experimental Age Groups was dressed *conservatively*, another was dressed *casually*, and the third was dressed *modishly*. The mode of dress included hair styles (beards included) and clothing. The clothing and hair styles were in keeping with recent definitions of the three terms. They were validated by asking a random sample of people to describe the dress for each of the models.

In summary, the final AAP instrument consisted of nine, eight by ten inch photographs of Young Adult, Middle Aged, and Elderly models posed in neutral positions in each of three dress styles. All subjects were caucasian and each picture was of a different individual. In each of the three Experimental Age Groups, there were photographs of one female and two males distributed.

ROLE REVERSAL PHOTOGRAPHS (RRP)

This set of pictures was composed of six photographs of role reversals in three settings: occupational (boss-employee), leisure, and counseling-teaching. There were two photographs in each of the three settings with posed activities in which the people in the pictures could be interpreted as performing acts which were unusual for their ages. The settings were defined enough that one could determine what general type of activity was taking place, but they were ambiguous enough that the roles people were playing could be perceived as reversed; that the younger person was performing a role usually filled by someone older and the older person was doing something more often associated with someone more youthful.

Occupational settings were selected on the basis of Neugarten's (1965) finding that her sample believed that by certain ages people should have decided upon a career and should have achieved their top job level. Some of Tuckman and Lorge's (1952) findings regarding stereotypes of older workers were also incorporated.

The leisure pictures consist of one scene at a cocktail party in which an older woman is arriving with an escort who is much younger than she. The other scene is a footrace in which the lead could be held by an older man. The cocktail party was selected because of the sanctions which the review of the literature suggested exist with respect to older people's dating and drinking habits (Neugarten, Moore and Lowe, 1965; Havinghurst and Albrecht, 1953). The footrace was chosen because it involved stereotypes of decreased physical capabilities and the belief that older people should taper off their competitive activities.

The counseling-teaching photographs were developed in order to ascertain groups' beliefs about the age of the person providing professional services. The teaching photograph shows a younger woman lecturing before an assembly of older people. In the second photograph, another young woman is seemingly counseling an older man and woman.

The final RRP were selected on the basis of two criteria: 1) the picture tended to suggest that the younger person was performing a role usually associated with an older person and the older person was likewise doing something unusual for his age; 2) in addition to being highly suggestive in the directions just described, the pictures were ambiguous enough that the roles could be interpreted either in keeping with age expectations or in keeping with the behavior being exhibited.

MODIFIED AAAT

The third instrument used was a modification of Kastenbaum's Age Appropriate Attitude Technique (1964). The modification was that attitude statements were made bisexual so that they might be associated with photographs of either males or females.

Procedure

Three female interviewers collected the data from the three Experimental Age Groups and each interviewed respondents from her own age group. This was done to encourage the participants to voice their age-based stereotypes, the assumption being that one would be more open with someone his own age.

Each interview was done individually usually in the subject's home. The interview lasted 1½ hours on the average. The first part of the interview consisted of the AAP and AAAT instruments. The second consisted of the RRP.

When the participant was seated at the table he was given the following general instructions to read:

> This is a study of how people form their initial impressions of strangers when they meet them for the first time. When you meet someone for the first time, you usually have some immediate thoughts about what he or she might be like. Later, your experiences with that person will either confirm or disprove them. But initially, you operate on your first impressions to decide whether you would like to know the person better; to decide how you think he or she might think, feel, or act and how you should act around him or her.
>
> There are two parts to this interview. First, you will be presented with *9* photographs of various people standing alone and you will state your initial impressions about them. Second, you will be shown a short series of *6* photographs showing people engaged in various activities and you will, as before, be asked to state your initial impression of what is occuring in the picture.
>
> The important factor in this interview is what your immediate reaction to the person is and how much you are able to determine from the available information. The accuracy of your impressions is not the concern of this study. Please give your *immediate reactions* and do not worry about their accuracy.
>
> For some of you, this may be the first time you have participated in this type of an activity. It does take time to become accustomed to working with the photographs. Therefore, there is no time limit. *Please feel free to work at your own pace and enjoy yourself.*

After the participant had read the paper, the AAP instrument was spread in front of him so that he could look at all the photographs at the same time. The interviewer then read the following instructions:

> In front of you there are photographs of several individuals who are probably strangers to you. If one is not a stranger, please tell me now as I must not count that answer.
>
> I want you to look at the pictures and consider each individually. In any order you want, take each photograph one at a time and 1) tell me what your immediate thoughts are about the person (what you think you know about the person) and 2) tell me what about the person's appearance made you think these things.
>
> Begin whenever you are ready.

When the participant began talking, the interviewer allowed a free flow of information and simply recorded the responses on code sheets which had one column for *cues*, one for *attributes*, and another for *strength*. There was one sheet for each picture and at the bottom of each there was a space for the interviewer to record any personal comments or any prompt questions she used.

The appearance items (clothes, posture, body size, age, etc.) which the subject used were recorded in the *cue column*. The characteristic (occupation, personality trait, etc.) which was associated with this cue was written in the *attribute column* next to the corresponding cue. The "sureness" or certainty with which the subject made the association was noted in the *strength column*. The sureness was taken to be the score given to the attribute when it was ranked along a five point scale in which a score of 1 = unsure, 2 = questionable, 3 = somewhat unsure, 4 = reasonably sure, and 5 = very sure.

If the participant had difficulty imputing characteristics to a model, the questions used to prompt him were:

1. "How would you describe this person to someone who was going to meet him/her for the first time?"
2. "Why did you select out these things as being important? What will these things tell the person about this stranger?"

After responding to all photographs, the participant was given a rating sheet which consisted of 9 separate rating blocks, one for each picture. Within these blocks, five possible cues were listed (dress, age, posture, facial expression, body size) along with one space where he could record anything he used but thought did not fall into one of the categories. He was asked to rank order the extent to which he used them from most to least. Next, all the Age Appearance Photographs were spread out, and he was told: "six of the nine people in these pictures have made statements regarding their outlooks on life and I would like to read them to you. Each statement was made by only one person and no person made more than one statement." The statements were from the modified AAAT.

The interview format for the second part of the interview was the same as for the first. The Role Reversal Photographs were spread out, and participant was told:

> In the photographs you will note various individuals are pictured in different social and work settings. I would like you to consider each photograph individually and in any order you wish. Please tell me 1) what you think is taking place and 2) what each individual is thinking and, or feeling at that moment.

For each of the six photographs there were two data recording sheets. The first consisted of a place to record the story the person told and any additional prompt questions which the interviewer may have used. The second sheet had three questions related to the photographs. First, "Do you think the situation shown in this photograph is unusual in any way? If yes, How?" Second, "did you have any difficulty in deciding what was taking place? If yes, why?" Third, "do you have any feelings of approval or disapproval about the behavior of the various people? Please explain what they are and why you feel this way."

Sample

Interviews were conducted with 90 volunteers from the Ann Arbor, Michigan area. Using Hollingshead's Two Factor Index of Social Position (1957), a sample was drawn such that within each Experimental Age Group of 30 the lower, middle, and upper socio-economic classes were equally represented. The $\bar{X}$-age of the Elderly Age Group was 70.4 years, the $\bar{X}$-age of the Middle Age Group was 48.0, and the $\bar{X}$-age of the Young Adult Group was 27.9 years. There were 20 females and 10 males in the Elderly Group, 19 females and 11 males in the Middle-Aged Group, and 18 females and 12 males in the Young Adult Group. None of the Elderly participants was institutionalized, some were living independently within a retirement village but they were able to care for themselves.

Results

Analyses were done to determine the answers to the following questions:

1. Compared to other sources of information, to what extent were the age cues considered when forming impressions of AAP models?
2. Were there differences between Experimental Age Groups or Socio-Economic Groups with respect to the extent age cues were utilized?
3. When the age of a person in a particular role does not necessarily coincide with expectation for that role, does the participant experience cognitive dissonance?
4. Among those who did perceive conflict, what did they believe was taking place; how was the conflict resolved? Among those who did not experience cognitive dissonance, what roles did they think the people in the picture were performing?
5. When participants were grouped by Age and SEC, were there any differences among them with respect to the amount of perceived conflict?

The coders utilized the following guidelines for collating the free flow response data collected with the AAP instrument. Any references to those items about the stranger's appearance such as jewelry, hair styles, and clothing were collated into a *Dress Cue* Category. References to the stranger's perceived age were categorized as *Age* Cues. Comments in reference to the expression on the stranger's face were categorized as *Facial Expression* Cues; references to the physiogamy which did not refer to expression were coded as *Facial Features*. *Body Build* Cues were references to the AAP model's physique and *Stance* Cues were references to the standing position.

When responses to all photographs were considered collectively, the following descending rank order according to use of cues evolved: dress, facial expression, age, body build, stance (see Tables 1 and 2). This held for all Experimental Age Groups and when participants rank ordered pre-selected cues visible in the photographs. Among the SEC Groups, the same rank order was seen, the only differences being that in the Upper SEC *Stance* and *Body Build* Cues were used qually. These rankings also evolved when each of the following were computed. These rankings also evolved when each of the following were computed:

1. the number of responses, regardless of the number of respondents, for each Cue Category, and for each photograph;
2. the mean amounts each Cue Category was used, calculated by dividing the number or respondents who used the particular Cue; and
3. the number of S's who used a Cue, regardless of the number of times each used it.

Table 1. Comparison of Age Groups with Respect to Number of References to Selected Appearance Cues

Age Group	Cue Categories																			
	Age		Dress		Resemblance to Someone		Facial Expression		Body Build		Hands		Stance		Facial Features		Sex		Balding	
	N	%	N	%	N	%	N	%	N	%	N	%	N	%	N	%	N	%	N	%
Young Adult	134	11.8	510	44.9	37	3.26	219	19.3	49	4.32	44	3.88	74	6.52	67	5.90	1	.001		
Middle Age	91	9.16	456	45.9	17	1.71	204	20.5	63	6.34	37	3.73	62	6.24	63	6.34				
Elderly	123	13.0	412	43.6	27	2.85	225	23.8	63	6.66	29	3.07	31	3.28	36	3.81			1	.001

Table 2. Comparison of Socio-Economic Groups with Respect to Number of References to Selected Appearance Cues

Socio-Economic Group	Cue Categories																			
	Age		Dress		Resemblance to Someone		Facial Expression		Body Build		Hands		Stance		Facial Features		Sex		Balding	
	N	%	N	%	N	%	N	%	N	%	N	%	N	%	N	%	N	%	N	%
Upper	150	13.0	501	44.0	38	3.35	237	20.9	60	5.28	38	3.35	60	5.28	52	4.58				
Middle	93	9.46	436	44.4	19	1.93	213	21.7	58	5.90	36	3.66	55	5.60	72	7.32	1	.001		
Lower	105	10.8	441	45.4	24	2.47	198	20.4	62	6.39	36	3.71	52	5.36	52	5.36			1	.001

When responses were considered by individual photographs, it became evident that all Experimental Age and SEC Groups utilized the perceived age of the model more when that model was Elderly (see Tables 3 and 4).

When participants were grouped according to the self-reported amount that they interacted with people from the three Experimental Age Groups, no significant differences were found with respect to the amount the age of the model was considered. Furthermore a comparison of the Strength Indexes suggested that the participants were, on the average, reasonably sure of all the characteristics which they imputed to the strangers. The results of the modified AAAT indicated similarity between the age of the AAP model associated with the statement and those ages Kastenbaum found were judged appropriate for the attitudes.

Table 3. Comparison of Age Groups—Number of References
to Selected Cues for Each AAP

Age groups	Appearance cues	Photographs—By Letter								
		A	B	C	D	E	F	G	H	I[a]
Young adults	Age	31	16	23	8	10	7	9	30	5
	Dress	42	92	35	54	50	67	68	45	66
	Resemblance		7	5	4	4	1	4	4	8
	Facial expression	21	24	41	18	23	21	22	26	23
	Body build	5	2	5	12	7	2	6	9	5
	Hands	4	4	2	7	1	7	12	7	
	Stance	13	6	13	11	3	9	1	14	13
	Facial features	6	6	10	4	5	15	11	5	5
	Sex				1					
Middle-aged	Age	29	6	12	5	3	6	5	19	6
	Dress	52	60	54	44	42	58	61	34	51
	Resemblance	1	1	3	3	2	1	1	4	1
	Facial expression	18	23	26	26	16	24	20	23	29
	Body build	4	1	4	19	11	5	8	8	4
	Hands	4	3	7	7	3		11	2	
	Stance	10	6	7	6	3	3	4	14	9
	Facial features	10	4	13	6		6	4	13	7
Elderly	Age	25	11	25	9	7	9	10	18	9
	Dress	40	41	46	45	46	42	55	35	52
	Resemblance	3	5	3	2	2	3	4	5	
	Facial expression	19	23	25	30	24	31	15	16	36
	Body build	3	2	9	23	6		14	4	2
	Hands	5	1	6	1	2	3	10		1
	Stance	9	2	3	5	6			5	1
	Facial features	3	2	5	2	5	6	5		8
	Balding						1			

[a] A, C, H = Elderly Models
B, E, I = Young Adult Models
D, F, G = Middle-Aged Models

Table 4. Comparison of Socio-Economic Classes—Number of
References to Selected Cues for Each AAP

Socio-economic groups	Appearance cues	Photographs—By Letter								
		A	B	C	D	E	F	G	H	I[a]
Upper socio-economic	Age	30	10	26	11	8	11	15	30	10
	Dress	49	63	45	52	53	61	72	36	70
	Resemblance	2	5	5	2	6	3	5	8	2
	Facial expression	26	24	36	25	26	27	23	23	27
	Body build	1	2	3	20	11	5	8	6	4
	Hands	4	2	6	3	2	5	12	4	
	Stance	11	7	6	8	5	4	2	11	6
	Facial features	4	6	6	4	3	7	6	8	8
Middle socio-economic class	Age	20	19	16	4	7	5	7	19	6
	Dress	37	64	45	44	40	49	32	41	54
	Resemblance	2	4	2	4	1	1	2	1	2
	Facial expression	15	28	31	23	18	24	15	24	35
	Body build	4	1	6	14	8	1	11	9	4
	Hands	6	5	6	4	2	2	9	1	1
	Stance	14	2	7	8	4	2	2	8	8
	Facial features	7	3	16	4	8	12	8	5	9
	Sex					1				
Lower socio-economic class	Age	35	10	18	7	5	6	2	18	4
	Dress	48	66	45	47	45	57	51	37	45
	Resemblance		4	4	3	1	1	2	4	5
	Facial expression	16	24	25	26	19	25	19	18	26
	Body build	7	2	9	20	5	1	9	6	3
	Hands	3	1	2	8	2	3	12	5	
	Stance	5	5	10	4	3	6	1	11	7
	Facial features	9	4	6	5		7	6	9	6
	Balding						1			

[a] A, C, H = Elderly Models
B, E, I = Young Adult Models
D, F, G = Middle-Aged Models

During the course of the AAP data analysis, a trend developed in which certain Cues tended to appear in single, conjoint associations with an attribute while others were used in groups of Cues which were all associated with a personality characteristic. It seemed that there was a difference between *Age* and other Cues in that *Age* was used in conjunction with other Cues more often than in single associations whereas other Cues seemed to appear most frequently in single associations. Thus, a Dependency Index was computed by classifying Cues as either Dependent or Independent. Those Cues which were used *alone* were coded as *Independent*; those used in conjunction with others were coded as *Dependent*.

Tables 5, 6, and 7, summarize the Dependent/Independent ratios for each AAP according to Age and SEC Groups. If one compares the Dependency ratios for each of the sets of photographs, the ratio remains the same for the

Table 5(a). Comparison of Dependency Indexes in Middle Age Photographs—Age Groups

		Pictures—By Letter											
		D				F				G			
Age groups	Dependency index	A	D	FE	BB	A	D	FE	S	A	D	FE	BB
Young adult	Dependent	6	10	6	1	7	20	3	2	9	12	8	2
	Independent	2	44	12	11		47	18	7		56	15	6
Middle-age	Dependent	5	10	4	5	5	12	10		4	10	5	4
	Independent		34	22	14	1	46	13	3	1	51	15	7
Elderly	Dependent	8	5	5	3	7	12	10		8	20	8	3
	Independent	1	40	25	20	2	30	21		2	35	7	6

Table 5(b). Comparison of Dependency Indexes in Middle Age Photographs—Socio-Economic Groups

		Pictures—By Letter											
		D				F				G			
Socio-economic groups	Dependency index	A	D	FE	BB	A	D	FE	S	A	D	FE	BB
Upper	Dependent	11	13	5	1	9	12	7	1	14	12	8	2
	Independent		39	20	19	2	49	20	3	1	60	15	4
Middle	Dependent	3	9	5	8	5	19	8		5	13	7	3
	Independent	1	35	18	6		30	16	2	2	51	8	5
Lower	Dependent	5	3	5		5	13	8	1	2	17	6	4
	Independent	2	44	21	20	1	42	17	5		34	13	10

Table 6(a). Comparison of Dependency Indexes in Young Adult Photographs—Age Groups

Age group	Dependency index	Pictures—By Letter												
		B					E				I			
		A	D	FE	R	S	A	D	FE	BB	A	D	FE	BB
Young adult	Dependent	14	12	3	2	1	7	10	10	3	4	11	3	1
	Independent	2	60	21	5	5	3	40	13	4	1	54	20	5
Middle age	Dependent	5	15	9		2	3	3	8	2	4	8	2	
	Independent	1	45	14	1	4		39	8	9	2	53	27	3
Elderly	Dependent	9	11	5	1		6	5	4	1	7	11	4	
	Independent	2	40	24	4	2	1	41	20	5	2	41	32	2

Table 6(b). Comparison of Dependency Indexes in Young Adult Photographs—Socio-Economic Groups

Socio-economic group	Dependency index	Pictures—By Letter												
		B					E				I			
		A	D	FE	R	S	A	D	FE	BB	A	D	FE	BB
Upper	Dependent	10	11	9	1	3	6	6	8	3	8	12	3	1
	Independent		52	15	4	4	2	47	18	17	2	58	24	3
Middle	Dependent	12	15	4	1		6	6	7	2	4	8	3	
	Independent	7	49	11	3	2	1	34	11	12	2	46	32	4
Lower	Dependent	6	12	4	1		4	6	7	1	3	10	3	
	Independent	4	54	12	3	5	1	39	12	1	1	35	23	3

Table 7(a). Comparison of Dependency Indexes in Elderly Photographs—Age Groups

		Pictures—By Letter														
		A					C					H				
Age group	Dependency index	A	D	FE	BB	S	A	D	FE	R	BB	A	D	FE	BB	R
Young adult	Dependent	29	12	2	1	9	18	4	10	1	2	28	12	8	4	1
	Independent	2	30	19	4	4	5	31	31	4	3	2	33	18	5	3
Middle age	Dependent	18	20	9	2	5	12	20	13		2	16	8	7	3	2
	Independent	11	32	9	2	5		34	13	3	2	3	26	16	5	2
Elderly	Dependent	7	2	3	1	4	23	10	8	1	4	16	7	2	2	2
	Independent	18	38	16	2	5	2	36	17	2	5	2	26	14	2	3

Table 7(b). Comparison of Dependency Indexes in Elderly Photographs—Socio-Economic Groups

		Pictures—By Letter														
		A					C					H				
Socio-economic group	Dependency index	A	D	FE	BB	S	A	D	FE	R	BB	A	D	FE	BB	R
Upper	Dependent	12	14	7		6	22	8	9		2	27	11	9	3	2
	Independent	18	32	19	1	5	4	37	27	5	1	3	25	14	3	6
Middle	Dependent	12	12	3	1	7	14	12	10	1	3	16	10	5	5	1
	Independent	7	25	12	3	7	2	33	21	1	3	3	31	19	4	
Lower	Dependent	20	8	4	3	5	17	14	12	1	3	17	6	3	1	2
	Independent	13	40	12	4		1	31	13	3	6	1	31	15	5	2

Middle Age and Young Adult photographs, but increases when Elderly photographs are considered. The ratio was 4/1 for pictures of models who were Young Adults and Middle Aged, but it was 7/1 for models who were Elderly. This is perhaps a reflection of the fact that more references were made to the *Age* of Elderly models and that the number of references to age does not seem to effect the Dependency Index. In other words, the tendency to use age in conjunction with other information was stronger than the tendency to use it in one to one associations with personality characteristics.

The reactions to the Role Reversal Photographs were analyzed in terms of cognitive dissonance. The participant was coded as experiencing *dissonance* if either in his free association responses or in his answers to the questions, he indicated that he thought the behavior of the people was unusual for their ages. If the participant indicated that he had such difficulty, his explanation of what was taking place in the picture was assumed to be his *resolution* of the perceived conflict between the ages and roles of the people.

The analysis of the data consisted of 1) isolating the central themes in the various stories, 2) separating those who experienced cognitive dissonance from those who did not, 3) comparing the stories of those perceiving conflict to those who did not, and 4) comparing Age and Socio-Economic Groups with respect to the number who experienced conflict. The *central theme* of a story was the preoccupation around which the participant established the relationship among the people in the picture. The rationale behind this analysis was that by grouping participants according to whether or not they perceived conflict, one essentially has two ends of a continuum. At one end, there are the responses of those people who acknowledged conflicting expectations because of the age of the actor and the role the picture implied he was playing. At the other end, there are the responses of those who did not experience conflicting expectations. If the majority resolved the conflict by leaving an actor in a role which conflicted with their expectations for a person that age, it would seem reasonable to assume that the age norms were not as strong as some other regulatory mechanism. If those who perceived conflict changed the roles of the actors to correspond to their age-based expectations, it would seem that age did have a strong regulatory effect upon allocation of certain roles. Furthermore, if there was congruence between stories of people who resolved the conflict by changing the role and the stories of those who did not perceive conflict it would seem that the age norms for that role may be stronger than in instances where the congruence did not exist.

The differences between the Experimental Age and Socio-Economic Groups were very small when they were compared with respect to the number who experienced cognitive dissonance. There was also not much variation in the resolutions they made. Therefore, in the final analysis the stories told by those who perceived conflict were compared to those who did not—regardless of their age or socio-economic background.

Teaching Photograph. Seventy-two participants did not experience any dissonance; 34 of these people related stories of a young teacher lecturing a class of older people. Eighteen experienced dissonance because the teacher was younger than the students but none of these people changed their RRP stories so that the younger person was not teaching. Tentatively, this implies that age is not a strong regulator mechanism of the teaching role.

Counseling Photograph. Sixty-four did not think anything was unusual about this picture. Thirty-one thought the younger woman was counseling the older couple about a family problem, 12 of these no-conflict participants thought the young girl was receiving advice from the older couple, and 11 said they thought this was an interview situation.

Sixteen of the dissonance participants resolved their perceived conflicts by leaving the young woman in the role of counselor, 8 thought the older people were counseling the young woman, and 2 thought it was an interview. Since the majority of the no-conflict participants also perceived the younger woman as the counselor, the results suggest that age was not a strong determinant of who should counsel whom.

Boss-Employee–Office Setting Photograph. Forty-two people experienced dissonance and 34 of these people resolved the perceived conflict between the ages and roles of the men by creating stories in which the older man was in charge of a business office. Forty-eight did not experience conflict and among these 16 thought the older man was the younger man's boss, 18 thought the younger man was giving professional advice, 8 thought the younger man was boss, and 4 thought the men were either colleagues or something was being bought or sold. When the stories of the two groups were compared, the results suggested that age was a regulator in this situation and that it was more acceptable for the younger man to be giving professional advice to an older man than it is for him to be advising the older man about business. This may be an indication of attitudes regarding the importance of experience on the ability to perform certain roles.

Boss-Employee–Construction Crew Photograph. Forty-five did not experience cognitive dissonance. Twenty-two of these thought the youngest man was crew boss and 16 thought the older man with glasses was in charge. There were also 45 who did report conflict. Twenty of them resolved the conflict by relating stories in which the older man was supervisor and 25 of them left the younger man in the supervisory role. Perhaps these results reflect the fact that it is more customary to see young men on construction cites and, therefore, age does effect the allocation of roles.

Runners–Leisure Photograph. There were 59 in the no-conflict group: 27 of them thought the picture showed a jogging club, 17 thought the older man was leading in a race, and the remainder thought he was either a coach or a father jogging with his sons. Thirty-one experienced dissonance, 16 of them thought the older man was leading the race because it was early and 12 said it was just a jogging club and not a race. Though there was no definite trend with respect to what was expected of the older man, there was a tendency to acknowledge the age of this man and expectations were centered around his perceived age and physical capabilities.

Cocktail Party—Leisure Photograph. Thirty-two people did not see anything unusual about an older woman and younger man arriving at a cocktail party together. Fifteen of these thought the woman was the man's mother, 10 thought the couple were dating, the remainder thought the couple were related or were fellow employees. Fifty-eight experienced dissonance; 23 of these people left the actors in dating roles, 16 said the couple were mother-son, and 13 thought they were related.

IMPLICATIONS OF RESULTS FOR FUTURE RESEARCH

Because this study was exploratory, the implications raised for future research are of primary importance. The following are some of the more important ones:

1. *Age* Cues were not used as often as others when these participants developed their initial impressions of the AAP models. This makes one question the value of determining how many misconceptions a person has as opposed to measuring what assumptions he acts upon. An attitude becomes more meaningful when one can measure its behavioral effects.

2. *Age* Cues were used in conjunction with other Cues (*dependently*) more often than *Dress, Facial Expression*, or the other Cues. Perhaps more data of this type should be collected and analyzed in terms of age-based attitudes which are *Independently* related to Age. If one does this, a scale could evolve which is representative of those attributes which are most strongly associated with chronological ages. This would help alleviate any previous age-based attitudes which were artifacts of the forced choice type of scaling utilized.

3. The results of the RRP data support the premise that chronological age is a dimension effecting the allocation of certain social roles. Once again, however, the extent to which it regulates allocation leads one to believe that more research is needed to determine the relative strength of its effect.

BIBLIOGRAPHY

Aaronson, B. S. Personality stereotypes of aging. *Journal of Gerontology*, 1966, 21, 458-462.

Altrocchi, J. and Eisdorfer, C. Comparison of attitudes toward old age, mental illness, and other concepts. In C. Tibbitts and W. Donahue (Eds.), *Aging around the world; Social and psychological aspects*. New York and London: Columbia University Press, 1962, pp. 860-865.

Aronson, E. and Mills, J. The effect of severity of initiation on liking for a group. *Journal of Abnormal and Social Psychology*, 1959, 59, 177-181.

Asch, S. E. Forming impressions of personality. *Journal of Abnormal and Social Psychology*, 1946, 41, 258-299.

Attneave, F. Some informational aspects of visual perception. *Psychological Review*, 1954, 61, 183-193.

Bekker, L. D. and Taylor, C. Attitudes toward the aged in a multi-generational sample. *Journal of Gerontology*, 1966, 21, 115-118.

Birdwhistell, R. L. Communication as a multi-channeled system. In D. L. Sills (Ed.), *International Encyclopedia of the Social Sciences*, 1967.

Birdwhistell, R. L. Kinesics and communication. In E. Carpenter and M. McIuhan (Eds.), *Exploration in communication*. Boston: Beacon Press, 1960.

Britton, J. and Britton, J. Discrimination of age by preschool children. *Journal of Gerontology*, 1969, 24, 457-460.

Bronfenbrenner, U. The study of identification through interpersonal perception. In R. Tagiuri and L. Petrullo (Eds.), *Person perception and interpersonal behavior*. Stanford: Stanford University Press, 1958, pp. 116-130.

Brunner, J. S. On perceptual readiness. *Psychological Review*, 1957, 64, 132-152.

Brunner, J. S. and Goodman, C. C. Value and need as organizing factors in perception. *Journal of Abnormal and Social Psychology*, 1947, 42, 33-44.

Brunner, J. S. and Postman, L. An approach to social perception. In Dennis and Wayne (Eds.), Current trends in social psychology. Pittsburg: University of Pittsburg Press, 1951, pp. 71-119.

Burgess, E. W. *Aging in western societies*. Chicago: University of Chicago Press, 1960.

Cohen, A. R. Cognitive tuning as a factor affecting impression formation. *Journal of Personality*, 1961, 29, 235-245.

Cottrell, L. Adjustment of the individual to his age and sex roles. *American Sociological Review*, 1942, 7, 617-620.

Duncan, K. J. Modern society's attitude toward aging. *Geriatrics*, 1966, 21, 217-222.

Eckman, P. Differential communication of affect by head and body clues. *Journal of Personality and Social Psychology*, 1965, 390-410.

Eckman, P. The repertoire of non-verbal behavior—categories, origins, usage and coding. University of California Press, 1967, 141-160.

Eckman, P. and Friesen, W. V. The repertoire of non-verbal behavior: Categories, origins, usage, and coding. *Semiotica*, Vol. 1, No. 1, 1969, pp. 50-98.

Eckman, P., Friesen, W. V., and Thompkins, S. S. Facial affect scoring technique: A first validity study. *Semiotica*, Vol. 3, No. 1, 1971, pp. 37-58.

Fast, J. *Body Language*. New York: Pocket Books, 1971.

Festinger, L. *A theory of cognitive dissonance*. New York: Harper and Row, 1957.

Frijda, N. H. Recognition of emotion. In L. Berkowitz (Ed.), *Experimental social psychology*, Vol. 4. New York: Academic Press, 1969, pp. 167-222.

Goffman, E. *Stigma*. Englewood Cliffs, New Jersey: Prentice-Hall, Inc., 1963.

Golde, P. and Kogan, N. A sentence completion procedure for assessing attitudes toward old people. *Journal of Gerontology*, 1959, 14, 355-363.

Havinghurst, R. J. and Albrecht, R. *Older People*. New York: Longmans, Green, 1953.

Hays, W. An approach to the study of trait implication and trait similarity. In R. Tagiuri and L. Petrullo (Eds.), *Person perception and interpersonal behavior*. Stanford: Stanford University Press, 1958, pp. 289-299.

Heider, F. Perceiving other people. In R. Tagiuri and L. Petrullo (Eds.), *Person perception and interpersonal behavior*. Stanford: Stanford University Press, 1958, pp. 22-40.

Henry, W. The thematic apperception technique in the study of groups and cultural problems. In H. Anderson and G. Anderson (Eds.), *An introduction to projective techniques*. New York: Prentice Hall, Inc., 1951, pp. 181-229.

Hollingshead, A. B. *Two factor index of social position*. New Haven: 1965 Yale Station, 1965.

Hunter, W. *Preparation for retirement*. Division of Gerontology Publication, University of Michigan, Ann Arbor, 1968.

Kastenbaum, R. and Durkee, N. Young people view old age. In R. Kastenbaum (Ed.), *New thoughts on old age*. New York: Springer Publishing Co., Inc., 1964. (a)

Kastenbaum, R. and Durkee, N. Elderly people view old age. In R. Kastenbaum (Ed.), *New thoughts on old age*. New York: Springer Publishing Co., Inc., 1964. (b)

Kastenbaum, R., Derbin, V., Sabatini, P., and Artt, S. "Ages of me": Toward personal and interpersonal definitions of functional aging. *Aging and Human Development*, 1972, 3, 197-212.

Kogan, N. Attitudes toward old people in an older sample. *Journal of Social Psychology*, 1961, 62, 616-622. (a)

Kogan, N. and Shelton, F. C. Beliefs about "old people": A comparative study of older and younger samples. *Journal of Genetic Psychology*, 1962, 100, 93-111.

Linton, R. *The cultural background of personality*. New York: Appleton-Century-Crofts, 1945.

Maxwell, R. J. and Silverman, P. Status information control and attitudes toward the aged: A cross-cultural study. *Gerontologist*, 1971, 11, No. 3, Pt. II, 35. (Abstract)

McDavid, J. W. and Harari, H. *Social Psychology*. New York: Harper and Row, Publishers, 1968.

McDavid, J. W. and Harari, H. Stereotyping of names and popularity in grade school children. *Child Development*, 1966, 37, 453-459.

Neugarten, B. L. and Gutmann, D. C. Age-sex roles and personality in middle age: A thematic apperception study. In B. L. Neugarten (Ed.), *Middle age and aging*. Chicago: University of Chicago Press, 1968, pp. 58-71.

Neugarten, B. L., Moore, J., and Lowe, J. Age norms, age constraints and adult socialization. *American Journal of Sociology*, 1965, 70, 710-717.

Neugarten, B. L. and Peterson, W. A. A study of the American age-grade system. *Proceedings of the 4th Congress of the International Association of Gerontology*, Vol. 3, 1957.

Peters, G. R. Self-conceptions of the aged, age identification and aging. *Gerontologist*, 1971, 11, No. 4, Pt. II, 69-73.

Riley, M. W. Social gerontology and the age stratification of society. *Gerontologist*, 1971, 11, 79-87.

Riley, M., Johnson, M., and Foner, A. *Aging and society*: Vol. 3, *A Sociology of age stratification*. New York: Russell Sage Foundation, 1972.

Rose, A. M. The Subculture of the Aging: A Topic for Sociologic Research. Gerontologists, 1962, 2, pp. 123-127.

Rosencranz, H. and McNevin, T. A factor analysis of attitudes toward the aged. *Gerontologist*, 1969, 9, 55-59.

Rosow, I. *Social integration of the aged*. New York: Free Press, 1967.

Sarbin, T. R. and Allen, V. Role theory. In G. Lindzey and E. Aronson (Eds.), *The handbook of social psychology*: Vol. 1. Massachusetts: Addison-Wesley Publishing Comp., 1968.

Secourd, P. F. Facial Features and inference processes in interpersonal perception. In R. Tagiuri and L. Petrullo (Eds.), *Person perception and interpersonal behavior*. Stanford: Stanford University Press, 1958, pp. 301-310.

Secourd, P. F., Dukes, W. F., and Bevan, W. Personalities in faces. I. An experiment in social perceiving. *Genetic Psychology Monograph*, 1954, 49, 231-279.

Shanas, E. *Older people in three industrial societies*. New York: Atherton Press, 1968.

Stein, D. D., Hardyck, J. A., and Smith, M. D. Race and Beliefs: An Open and Shut Case. Journal of Personality and Social Psychology, 1965, 1, pp. 281-289.

Tagiuri, R., Kogan, N., and Brunner, J. S. The transparency of interpersonal choice. Sociometry, 1955, 18, 624-635.

Tagiuri, R. and Petrullo, L. *Person perception and interpersonal behavior*. Stanford: Stanford University Press, 1958.

Teresa, J. The measurement of meaning as interpreted by teachers and students in visuo-gestural channel expressions through nine emotional expressions. Unpublished Doctoral Dissertation. University of Michigan, 1971.

Traxler, A. J. Intergenerational differences in attitudes toward old people. *Gerontologist*, 1971, 11, No. 3, Pt. II, 34. (Abstract)

Triandis, H. C. and Triandis, L. M. Some studies of social distance. In I. Steiner and M. Fishbein (Eds.), *Current trends in social psychology*. New York: Holt, Reinhart, and Winston, Inc., 1966, pp. 207-217.

Tuckman, J. and Lorge, I. Attitudes toward old workers. *Journal of Social Psychology*, 1953, 37, 249-260.

Tuckman, J. and Lorge, I. Attitudes toward old workers. *Journal of Applied Psychology*, 1952, 36, 149-153.

Wells, W. D., Goi, F. J., and Seader, S. A Change in the Product Image. Journal of Applied Psychology, 1958, 2, pp. 120-121.

Wood, V. D. Age Appropriate Behavior for Older People. Gerontologists, 1971, 2:4(II), pp. 74-78.

Zajonc, R. B. The process of cognitive tuning in communication. *Journal of Abnormal and Social Psychology*, 1960, 61, 159-167.

part three

PERSONALITY: CHANGE AND CONTINUITY OVER THE LIFE COURSE

chapter 8

EGO FUNCTIONING IN OLD AGE: EARLY ADULT LIFE ANTECEDENTS[1]

Joseph A. Kuypers, Ph.D.

It seems natural in the course of the mind's reflections to wonder about whether one's personal and cultural past creates the forms and actions of the moment. Why do I experience life as I do? What formed my particular personality and ideology? And what part does the sharing of common genetic messages with my family play? Academic and theoretical answers to these questions—each in its own way seeking to understand the influences of the past and its explanations of future and present—has taken many forms. Archetypes transmit psychological dispositions, genes transmit messages of size, shape, and color, early material or maternal deprivations effect later emotionality and psychological health. Early advantages of health and economics determine later aspects of adaptability and personal strength. The parenting styles experienced in childhood determine subsequent character and philosophy. Historical emphases of value, custom, and ideology are taught, absorbed, and changed. These, in part, determine behavior of the present, demanding that new forms of thought and action spring from older forms. Each of these explanations defines its own boundaries and tries to measure its influence against that of others—genetics vs. environment—race vs. culture—personal reinforcement histories vs. free will.

The debates over which has the stronger influence seem never-ending

[1] Supported by USPHS Grant HD-03617, Intergenerational Studies in Development and Aging, at The Institute of Human Development.

suggesting that the debate itself is a common denominator of how we seek to know the power of the past. The least this debate demonstrates is that the past is, indeed, powerful. Certain families cripple the early growth of children and create persistent, self-defeating orientations to the world. Psychotherapies struggle to free a person from the effects of disadvantaged or debilitating pasts. Critical periods of early life pattern pathways of all subsequent development, as when environmental deprivation defines the worlds of infants. Habits, patterns of thought and action, personal styles, traits, idiosyncracies, are but a few of the many constructs used to describe the behavioral and ideological residues of the past.

For persons interested in what old age is to present, debates over the influence of past have a special allure. With more years of life passed, experiences of early life become more distant. Are their effects less persistent? Does the long term repetition of behavior lead to a firmer hold on personal style or attitude? When is this comforting, when self-defeating? Are the influences of emergent values and changes in cultural style less influential on the minds of older persons? For better or worse? As the culture notices its elderly, characteristics and styles of aging are defined. To be old (some say) is to be conservative. To be old is to lose the capacity to change and grow. Some elderly age gracefully, some not. Some lose the strength of their body, some not. Some find the potentials and joys of aging in all they touch, while others lose energy and seem to wait for death. Old age is a time for some when levels of meaning are more profound yet others sink into a deep despair and depression. The variations in the courses of aging are many and often speak to deeply rooted concerns of people: contact with the world of people; ability to see, walk, hear, and think; desire to live and usefulness to the world; being dependently needy yet unwanted.

So the prospects of how one ages are not inconsequential to people. They speak to the personal concerns of all of us and prompt profound thought about life and equally profound questions about past. Answers to the question "What determines aging?"—as with all questions of past—take many forms: genetics, environment, losses of family and friends, mental change, and psychological habit, among others play their part. Furthermore, the search for answers to this question has taken many forms. Personal memoirs and diaries, life reviews and autobiographies reach back in memory and reveal themes and patterns of the life course. Contrasts of older people in different periods of time or other nations yield information about the influence of history and culture. Comparisons of longevity rates, diseases, and biological structures between siblings and twins give cues to the power of genetics on the aging process. Comparisons between the young and old tell something of the combined effects of developmental age, peer group memberships, and history. One would hope that the combined effects of these analyses will be to better understand and thereby gain some mastery over conditions which create a personally rewarding and healthful aging.

This hope has been my guidepost in thinking about and exploring aging. I have sought to inquire into aspects of older peoples' lives which relate to psychological health, to the ability to draw from one's world in ways that enhance effectiveness and emotional health. In an ongoing study of personality and lifestyle among 142 elderly persons, (Maas and Kuypers, 1974) it is apparent that wide variations exist in coping ability, in accuracy of perception of environmental expectations, and in the ability to mediate between inner need and those expectations. Some in this study group seem closed to their world, to distort both what is perceived and what is desired. They seem propelled by the past and in consequence, brittle in the face of change. Others seem more flexible in their approach to their environment. They maintain an openness to thought and an empathic sense of others, and more closely match a model of flexible competence. Not surprisingly, the former seem more defensive and less satisfied with their lives. They suffer more physical distress and often experience the world as operating *on* them, as composed of forces outside their control which impinge upon them. The latter, more self-satisfied and free from fearful anticipations, sense their own mastery over their world and act upon it with the confidence of having an impact (Kuypers, 1972). With this observation of such differences in psychological style, a natural question eme rges: are there aspects of past which seem to influence or pattern these different capacities and experiences in old age? Are persons who in old age show greater adaptability experiencing the rewards of earlier economic or career advantages? or better health or closer and more enduring friendships and marriages?

I have the rare opportunity, as a researcher, to study such questions as these rather directly. I have data (of course limited in focus and method) on old age parents when they were young adults, 40 years ago. These early adult life data cover a wide range: including measures and indexes of intelligence, health, education and economics, marital relations, and personality when our study subjects were young adults (average age around 30 years). They encourage the following questions:

1. Do variations in coping ability in old age show any connections to aspects of past over 40 years of the adult life line?

2. Are these connections stronger for some aspects of young adulthood such as personality or health but not economics or family relations?

3. Are there alternative notions of coping ability in old age, some of which seem more rooted in or more determined by past than others?

   Some define adaptability by the presence or absence of negative or pathological behaviors. In this model, a person is confused or delusional or he is not. Others define adaptability as the presence or absence of positive capacities, as when a person is empathic or not, logical or not. Do these different conceptions of adaptability or coping ability, one based on pathology, one on strength have different connections to past? Is pathology in old age rooted to environmental deprivations of young adulthood, for example, while strength finds connections to earlier intimacies and friendships?

4. And finally, to what degree to aspects of intelligence, health, economics, personality and family interaction, this time measured in *old age*, relate to high levels of coping, defense and disorganization?

These are the questions the following research is designed to address.

THE PRESENT STUDY: YOUNG ADULT ANTECEDENTS
OF EGO FUNCTIONING IN OLD AGE

The specific intent of this study is to examine the nature and strength of association between aspects of behavior and environment in young adulthood and variations in adaptive capacity in old age. If a complete map of the adult life progressions which lead to adaptability in old age could be developed, analysis would focus on many periods of adult life and would consider the relative impact of a variety of social and personal issues. Any study must, as this one does, fall far short of this expanded life course analysis, yet each smaller contribution adds to the larger effort. This study examines the relationship of variations in *health, intelligence, economics, personality*, and *family interaction* in young adulthood to variations in ego capacities in old age. The same group of 95 elderly persons (71 women and 24 men drawn from a larger sample of 142; see Maas and Kuypers, 1974) were studied 40 years ago when they were young parents of infant children.

Early Adult Life Data

In 1929-30 a team of researchers (see Jones et al., 1971) at the University of California, Berkeley, began what was to become a large scale longitudinal study of development from infancy to middle age. As part of early data collection procedures, the then young parents (mean age 30 years) of the infant subjects were observed and interviewed. Contact was maintained with these parents during the first 18 years of their child's life, although most of the data available for this study are limited to one point in early adulthood, when the infant subjects were 21 months old. The data collected on the young parents in 1929-30 represents a wide range. Although hindsight would argue for different measures now, as a researcher of the 1970's looking back to the early phases of the longitudinal study, one is impressed by the breadth of information gathered. Previously gathered information covers 5 areas: 1. intellectual capacity, 2. health status, 3. socioeconomic and work related issues, 4. personality, and 5. social-interaction and family relations. These data (a total of 68 measures for women and 50 for men) provide the information against which ego-functioning variations in old age will be analyzed. (For a fuller description of the particular measures in the early antecedent data set, see Macfarlane, 1938.)

Aging Parent Data

In 1969-70, the now aging parents (mean age 70 years) were once again interviewed and tested. A wide range of social interaction, personality, and contextual information was gathered to study the major lifestyles and personality organizations exhibited in the larger sample of 142 parents. While 142 parents were interviewed in 1969-70, only 95 parents (24 men and 71 women) are included in this analysis. This reduction from 142 to 95 is created by the absence of early adult life data on some of the 142 parents. For some of the correlations being reported, even smaller numbers of parents have complete data both early and late in this study's history.

Variations in Ego Functioning in Old Age

One major focus of the Maas and Kuypers analysis was the organization of personality as described by the 100-item California Q-sort (Block, 1971). Factor analysis of Q-sort profiles yielded 7 personality groups, 4 for women and 3 for men. These 7 groups showed substantial variations in adaptive capacity as defined by levels of ego functioning. Certain parents were characterized by ego disorganization while others (by far the majority) were notably high on coping ability. Further, those parents whose personality organization was marked by tension, fearfulness, or constriction seemed most firmly rooted to earlier ways of being 40 years ago. In many respects, the early adulthood associations to personality in old age demonstrated a high degree of continuity of personality over time, especially for parents whose personality in old age seemed marginally adaptive. These data suggested that the adult-life trajectory for the eventual development of personality tension or disorganization in late life was more firmly established than that for personality strength. One question raised by this analysis was whether the historical roots of extremes in adaptability (this time defined by ego functioning) followed a similar path. That is, are persons in old age who show ego disorganization more "locked on" to a difficult life course than persons high on coping ability? Are the early adult life antecedents of high adaptability less apparent than the antecedents of low adaptability?

Adaptive Capacity Defined

Adaptive capacity in old age is operationally defined in terms of ego functioning. An interesting and sensitive understanding of ego capacity is provided by the distinction between *coping, defense*, and *disorganized* behavior developed by Norma Haan (1969). Coping behavior in its most general sense, is considered flexible and self-adaptive. It represents an approach to the world marked by a fluid responsiveness to external and internal states. People noted for their coping ability are in touch with what is coming as well as what is past. In short, they have a firm, but flexible, hold on their reality and can act in self-directed ways. *Defensive behavior* in contrast, is somewhat compelled and rigid. It may represent an expression of personal style which, though familiar and practised to the individual, does not allow a realistic, tempered appraisal of reality. It appears to be behavior which is pushed from the past, requiring a "fit" between what is perceived in the "now" and one's personal response. To accomplish this "fit," distortion of the present may be required, allowing personal balance at the expense of a firm, flexible grounding in reality. And finally, *disorganized behavior* is just that, disorganized. It is unmodulated and often unrelated to a public sense of what is happening.

Table 1 shows that 10 measures are subsumed under the coping, defense, and disorganization categories. Also shown are the 10 ego *processes* which cross-cut all levels of ego functioning. For example, individual measures of empathy (coping), projection (defense) and ideas of reference (disorganization) all involve "degrees of sensitive awareness" to other's often unexpressed feelings or ideas. The 30 ego functioning measures are, therefore, organized in two ways. The coping, defense, and disorganization distinction captures alternative ways adaptability has been operationally and theoretically defined. Defensiveness subsumes many of the classic defense mechanisms developed by Anna Freud (1966). These are concepts often used in the description of neurotic behavior. Disorganization, in contrast, deals more with pathological behavior and subsumes concepts often used in describing psychosis. Coping behaviors echo many of the concepts used in defining mental health, efficacy, or self actualization (see Smith, 1968). In short, each of these ego distinctions represents alternative ways of defining adaptability.

The second organization of the 30 ego measures serves to distinguish 10 ego processes, each of which cross-cuts the alternative definitions of adaptability. As defined by Norma Haas, 4 ego operations cluster the 10 ego processes; 3 relate to *cognitive* operations, 3 relate to *self-reflective* operations, 3 relate to *affective* operations, and one to *attention-focusing* operations. Analysis over time will determine which, if any, of these four ego operations have particularly strong associations over time. Are affective operations more or less connected to young adulthood behaviors than, for example, cognitive operations? Further, where are the over time connections strongest? To early adultlife intellectual status, to health, to personality, to socioeconomic status, or to family interactions?

Correlations are reported between young adulthood measures and the 30 ego functioning measures in old age. A first set of correlations reports the over time associations between the coping, defense, and disorganization summary measures (numerical summary of 10 measures), and all antecedent measures. This analysis will contrast the direction and strength of association for the alternative

Table 1. Operations and Processes for Three Definitions of Adaptability

Ego operations	Ego processes	Adaptability[a] Defined as		
		Coping	Defense	Disorganization
Cognitive Operations	discrimination	objectivity	isolation	tangentiality
	detachment	intellectuality	intellectualization	neologisms
	end-means symbolization	logical analysis	rationalization	confabulation
Self-reflective Operations	delayed response	tolerance of ambiguity	doubt	immobilization
	selective awareness	concentration	denial	hebrephrenic
	temporal reversals	regression in service of ego	regression	decompensation
Attention-focusing Operations	sensitivity	empathy	projection	delusional
Affective Operations	impulse diversion	sublimation	displacement	impulse preoccupation
	impulse transformation	substitution	reaction formation	unstable alteration
	impulse restraint	suppression	repression	depersonalization, withdrawal

[a] Each of the 10 measures subsumed under coping, defense and disorganization are 1 to 5 point ratings made by a minimum of 2 clinically trained raters on transcripts of 3 to 6 hour interviews. Inter-rater reliability is reported elsewhere (Maas and Kuypers, 1974).

definitions of old age adaptability. A second correlational analysis determines whether certain ego operations have more firmly visible antecedents.

Hunches

Depending on one's perspective, various arguments could be developed for which of the five aspects of young adulthood would relate most to late life adaptability. Variations in intellectual or cognitive abilities could be assumed to provide the foundation for the development of adaptive capacities in old age. Correspondingly one might suggest that early adult life health disadvantage would deter adult development. For those who look to conditions of environment and social structure, aspects of economics, career, and educational achievements would seem to provide the foundation for adaptive development late in life. Yet, many clinicians and personality theorists would look to early adult life differences in personality or mood or self-view to explain variations in later adult development. And finally, some stage theorists would argue (notably Erikson, 1950; Havighurst, 1949; and Peck, 1960) that failures in one's ability to establish a close and intimate interpersonal world would predict further adult life course failures.

According to Erikson, the stage of young adulthood (roughly that period of life our aging parents were in 40 years ago) involves issues of intimacy and isolation. For persons who avoid experiences of close friendship, physical contact, and self-abandonment in sexual union, subsequent development may be marked by a "deep sense of isolation and consequent self-absorption" (Erikson, 1950, p. 229). A loose interpretation of Erikson's argument in terms of the present study would predict that difficulties and tensions in the young marriages of our parents 40 years ago would relate to the eventual development of ego-disorganization and perhaps ego-defensiveness. Failure at one stage predicts failure at the next, but success does not predict success, since success is also dependent on subsequent stages of middle age generativity and old age ego integrity. In terms of this study, one might argue from a stage perspective, that variations in early marriage and interpersonal relations will relate to the presence or absence of ego disorganization or defensiveness in old age, but not coping ability.

Characteristics of the Sample

As reported more fully elsewhere (see Kuypers, 1972 and Maas and Kuypers, 1974) the parents represent a fairly advantaged group. All of the fathers are married and living with their spouse, while two thirds of the mothers share their homes with spouse. While some parents report minor self-care difficulties (approximately one third), none are so incapacitated as to be unable to live in the community; 85% of fathers and 68% of mothers live in one-family housing and only a small fraction (4% of fathers and 10% of mothers) live in old-age segregated housing. The parents of this study have substantial formal education. Of the fathers, 53% have completed college and 83% have at least a high school diploma. For the mothers, 74% have completed high school and 32% have college diplomas. And finally, the parents themselves consider their financial situation fairly advantageous; 77% of the fathers and 66% of the mothers consider their income to be above average.

RESULTS

Antecedents of Adaptability: Coping, Defense, Disorganization

Table 2 presents the percentage of significant associations, sexes separately, between the three components of adaptability in old age (coping, defense, and disorganization) and the five areas of behavior and status covered in the early adulthood data (intelligence, health, socioeconomic status, personality, and marriage). As one focuses on the five areas of antecedent behavior and status, some stand out as having over time associations to ego functioning in old age, others not. Early adult life *health status* is poorly associated over time. For the men, variations in early life health status do not show any associations over time

Table 2. Percentage of Young Adulthood Measures Significantly Associated to Coping, Defense, and Disorganization Summary Scores in Old Age

	Number of measures[a]	% Significant Associations to Adaptability Defined as		
		Coping	Defense	Disorganization
Men (n of 24)				
Area				
Health	5	0	0	0
Socioeconomic	16	19	0	38
Personality	10	0	20	0
Marriage	19	5	5	5
Total	50	8	6	14
Women (n of 71)				
Area				
Intelligence	5	80	20	20
Health	4	0	25	25
Socioeconomic	14	36	0	22
Personality	24	13	4	4
Marriage	21	5	20	40
Total	68	20	12	21

[a] These antecedent measures have been described fully in various publications throughout the years of the Institute of Human Development longitudinal studies. For most complete descriptions, see Macfarlane, (1938).

to coping, defense, or disorganization. For the women, one measure of health (out of four) shows associations of significant proportions, and in this case, only to defensive or disorganized behavior in old age. Nor are the over time associations strong between early adult life *personality* and ego capacity in late life. It is entirely possible however, that these aspects of behavior are indeed powerful determinants of life course development and that other measures in early adult life or others in late life would show a greater strength of connection. Our data, however, show these aspects of young adulthood to be least connected to ego functioning in old age.

The over time associations between intelligence, socioeconomic status, and marital relationships, on the other hand, present quite a different picture. For the women, early adult life variations in intellectual capacity are highly correlated to late life, especially when the over time focus is on ego coping in late life (early estimates of intellectual capacity are not available for the men). Further, *socioeconomic status* shows a consistently high degree of association for both men and women over time, but primarily in regard to aspects of ego coping and disorganization, but not defensiveness. And finally, variations in *marital and family relations* in early adulthood show substantial over time associations, more so for the women and more so when the focus is on ego disorganization in late life. In summary, therefore, these data suggest that aspects of young adulthood do, indeed, relate to aspects of ego functioning in old age, but that the strength of association depends on 1) the gender of the subject, 2) the model of adaptability used to define ego functioning in old age, and 3) the specific area of early adulthood under consideration.

Sex of Subject

Contrasts between men and women in this study must be understood in the light of differences in sample size (24 men and 71 women) and the limited range of antecedent data available for men. In general, over time associations are greater for women than men, although this could be an artifact of sample size alone. Secondly, women seem to have a greater over time association between marriage and family interaction and late life ego capacity. These data very tentatively suggest that variations in marriage and family life are more critical for women than men in determining variations in late life ego capacities.

Model of Adaptability

Inspection of Table 2 shows quite clearly that the three models of adaptability (coping, defense, and disorganization) have different early adult life antecedents. Variations in old age *coping* ability seem most directly related to variations in intellectual and socioeconomic status in early adult life. It seems as if the conception of adaptability which rests on positive conceptions of mental health, or efficacy, or self-actualization are rooted in aspects of intellectual capacity and environmental limitations or advantages. When the focus is on coping ability in old age, failures or successes in young marriage, or early health, or personality do not seem connected over time. Variations in *disorganization* in old age (adaptability defined by pathology) show quite a different over time rootedness. In this case, old age ego disorganization seems most connected to socioeconomic status (as with coping behavior in old age) *and* variations in marriage and family in young adulthood. Aspects of interpersonal life, of intimacy and personal bond assume greater over time impact *if* adaptability is defined in terms of ego failures. Variations in defensiveness in old age (adaptability defined by defense mechanisms) seem to be minimally connected to early adult life behavior. Socioeconomic status in early adult life is not associated to defensiveness in old age, as it was with both coping and disorganization. Further, only minimal associations between defensiveness are apparent to personality, health and intelligence in young adulthood. In other words, it appears that the over time connections in adulthood are strongest when adaptability is defined in terms of strength (coping) or failure (disorganization), but not defensiveness.

Specific Area of Early Adulthood Under Consideration

These data suggest that over time associations are strongest for aspects of socioeconomic status, intelligence, and marriage and the family, but weakest for aspects of personality and health. Socioeconomic status has the most broad banded over time associations in the respect that it appears for both men and women, and it relates to both coping and disorganization behavior in late life. Intelligence is most strongly rooted (in terms of per cent of significant associations) but is limited to over time associations to coping behavior in women for whom early intellectual data is available. And marriage and family interaction is related over time, but most strongly to aspects of disorganization in old age and most strongly for women.

SPECIFIC ANTECEDENT MEASURES WHICH RELATE TO COPING, DEFENSE AND DISORGANIZATION IN OLD AGE

Table 3 shows the antecedent measures which are significantly correlated with the summary measures of coping, defense, and disorganization.

Significant Coping Antecedents

For the women (data is available only for the women), four measures (80% of all possible) of early adult life *intellectual capacity* relate to coping ability in old age. All associations show that high levels of coping behavior in old age are

Table 3. Significant Antecedents to Coping, Defense, and Disorganization Summary Scores

Women (n of 71)	Men (n of 24)

SIGNIFICANT COPING ANTEDECENTS[a]

Intelligence (5 measures)
higher estimated level of intellectual
  capacity ($r \leqslant .42$, $p \leqslant .001$)
greater mental alertness ($r \leqslant .42$, $p \leqslant .001$)
greater speed of mental processes
  ($r \leqslant .34$, $p \leqslant .05$)
more accurate use of language
  ($r \leqslant .44$, $p \leqslant .001$)

Intelligence (no measures)

no data on intelligence for men

Health (4 measures)
no significant associations

Health (5 measures)
no significant associations

Socioeconomic status (14 measures)
more education ($r \leqslant .41$, $p \leqslant .001$)
more moves from birth of Child to 18th
  birthday ($r \leqslant .28$, $p \leqslant .05$)
lower average financial strain from
  birth to 18th birthday ($r \leqslant .48$, $p \leqslant .001$)
higher index of social class (ICS) at birth of
  Child ($r \leqslant .42$, $p \leqslant .001$)

Socioeconomic status (16 measures)
more education ($r \leqslant .24$, $p \leqslant .05$)
lower average financial strain from birth of
  Child to 18th birthday ($r \leqslant .41$, $p \leqslant .05$)
higher occupation level ($r \leqslant .35$, $p \leqslant .05$)

Personality (24 measures)
greater poise ($r \leqslant .25$, $p \leqslant .05$)
more cheerful ($r \leqslant .30$, $p \leqslant .05$)
more open ($r \leqslant .31$, $p \leqslant .05$)

Personality (10 measures)
no significant associations

Marriage and Family (21 measures)
more sex instruction given to Child
  ($r \leqslant .41$, $p \leqslant .01$)

Marriage and Family (19 measures)
less conflict with relatives ($r \leqslant .66$, $p \leqslant .001$)

SIGNIFICANT DEFENSE ANTECEDENTS

Intelligence (5 measures)
less mental alertness ($r \leqslant .27$, $p \leqslant .05$)

Intelligence (no measures)

Health (4 measures)
poorer present health ($r \leqslant .35$, $p \leqslant .05$)

Health (5 measures)
no significant associations

Socioeconomic status (14 measures)
no significant associations

Socioeconomic status (16 measures)
no significant associations

Personality (24 measures)
more worrisome ($r \leqslant .27$, $p \leqslant .05$)

Personality (10 measures)
poorer social adjustment ($r \leqslant .43$, $p \leqslant .05$)
more withdrawn ($r \leqslant .43$, $p \leqslant .05$)

Marriage and Family (21 measures)
lower marital compatibility
  ($r \leqslant .36$, $p \leqslant .05$)
lower adjustment to spouse ($r \leqslant .38$, $p \leqslant .05$)
lower friendliness to spouse ($r \leqslant .35$, $p \leqslant .05$)
less closeness to Child ($r \leqslant .35$, $p \leqslant .05$)
less friendliness to child ($r \leqslant .40$, $p \leqslant .01$)

Marriage and Family (19 measures)
less sex instruction given to Child
  ($r \leqslant .53$, $p \leqslant .01$)

Table 3. (cont.)

Women (n of 71)	Men (n of 24)
SIGNIFICANT DISORGANIZATION ANTECEDENTS	
Intelligence (5 measures) less mental alertness ($r \leqslant .35, p \leqslant .01$)	*Intelligence* (no measures)
Health (4 measures) poorer present health ($r \leqslant .30, p \leqslant .05$)	*Health* (5 measures) no significant associations
Socioeconomic status (14 measures) lower age ($r \leqslant .25, p \leqslant .05$) greater age difference between self and husband ($r \leqslant .32, p \leqslant .01$) more financial strain, birth to 18th birthday of Child ($r \leqslant .32, p \leqslant .05$)	*Socioeconomic status* (16 measures) less education ($r \leqslant .34, p \leqslant .05$) greater education difference between self and wife ($r \leqslant .39, p \leqslant .05$) lower Warner Index of Social Class at birth of Child ($r \leqslant .45, p \leqslant .01$) lower Warner Index of Social Class at 18th birthday of Child ($r \leqslant .60, p \leqslant .01$) lower occupational level at Child birth ($r \leqslant .49, p \leqslant .01$) lower occupational level at 18th birthday of Child ($r \leqslant .41, p \leqslant .05$)
Personality (24 measures) less freshness ($r \leqslant .20, p \leqslant .05$)	*Personality* (10 measures) no significant associations
Marriage and Family (21 measures) lower marital compatibility ($r \leqslant .36, p \leqslant .05$) poorer adjustment to spouse ($r \leqslant .44, p \leqslant .01$) less friendliness to spouse ($r \leqslant .40, p \leqslant .01$) more conflict over recreation ($r \leqslant .39, p \leqslant .10$) more conflict over management of money ($r \leqslant .42, p \leqslant .01$) less agreement over expenditures ($r \leqslant .40, p \leqslant .01$) more conflict over discipline of children ($r \leqslant .39, p \leqslant .01$) higher discrepant educational interests for Child ($r \leqslant .34, p \leqslant .05$)	*Marriage and Family* (19 measures) less sex instruction given to Child ($r \leqslant .47, p \leqslant .05$)

[a] Significant correlations are reported relative to high levels of coping, defense or disorganization.

related to high estimated intellectual capacity, high mental alertness, high speed of mental process, and accurate use of language in young adulthood. These data indicate that cognitive or intellectual capacity, defined in various ways, provides at least one pathway to the eventual development of coping ability in old age. In short, intellectual potentials in early life appear to have a stronger impact on adaptability in old age, when defined as ego coping behavior.

As already noted, no over time associations between early adult life *health status* and ego capacity in old age are apparent for either men or women. It may well be, however, that health status does have a substantial impact in the adult life cycle, but that variations in our sample 40 years ago (or the specific measures used for assessment) did not tap a wide enough range to reveal the impact of somatic variations on late life behavior. In light of the superior health of the subjects in old age, one might expect equal uniformity in health 40 years ago.

As with intelligence in young adulthood, *socioeconomic* associations to coping in late adult life are in the expected direction. More education, minimal financial strain, and high levels of socioeconomic status (as well as high geographic mobility) relate to high levels of coping ability in old age. Apparently the environmental advantages represented by income and education bode well for the eventual development of high coping ability in old age. Clearly, the eventual benefits for older persons of a relatively advantaged early adult life is underscored in this data.

Three measures (13% of the total possible) of *personality* in young adulthood are associated with coping ability in old age for the women, none for the men. Greater poise, cheerfulness, and openness to discussion are positively correlated with the greater coping ability for our elderly women.

And finally, as with the personality measures in young adulthood, there is little evidence that variations in *marriage and family life* of the young parents relates to variations in coping capacity in old age. Rather, taking all antecedent data together, the life cycle trajectory of coping ability in old age seems most related to aspects of socioeconomic advantage and intelligence in young adulthood.

Significant Defense Antecedents

Table 3 shows that aspects of intelligence, health, socioeconomic status and personality do not show over time associations to defensiveness in old age to any substantial degree. In only one area, and only for the women, are associations present. In this case, low marital compatibility, poor adjustment between husband and wife, relatively high hostility to husband, and a distant-hostile relationship to their study child all relate to the development of high defensiveness in old age. As Erikson predicted, failures in interpersonal relations in young adulthood appear related to negative aspects of personality (in this case ego defensiveness) in old age.

Significant Disorganization Antecedents

The over time association of difficulty in the early life marriages of the subjects noted above in regard to defensiveness is even stronger when adaptability is defined by ego disorganization (but again only for the women in our sample). In this case, aspects of relations with husband indicate that a distant bond to husband and hostilities between husband and wife relate to ego disorganization in old age. Further, there is considerable evidence that conflict over recreation, money management, discipline of children, and money expenditures relate to high levels of ego disorganization in old age. In contrast to the over time associations to defensiveness, however, these data do not suggest that relations with children relate to disorganization. Rather, the trajectory to disorganization in old age (in terms of its interpersonal roots) seems to involve more exclusively relations with husband.

The over time impact of socioeconomic variations in early adulthood to late life disorganization is equally apparent, but most for the men. While 22% of all possible socioeconomic measures are significantly associated with ego disorganization for women, 38% are significant for the men. Low levels of socioeconomic status, limited amounts of education, non-professional or laboring careers, and a large difference between spouse educational levels relates to ego disorganization in old age for the men.

Over-Time Associations to 10 Ego Processes

Data so far presented has focused on the early antecedent associations to summary measures of coping, defense, and disorganization in old age. Each of the summary measures is composed of scores on 10 individual ego-process measures which, in turn, are subsumed by 4 ego operations. Do associations over time appear stronger for some ego operations, but not others?

Table 4 shows the average number of significant correlations between each ego operation (cognitive, self-reflective, attention-focusing, and affective) and all early antecedent measures (68 for women and 50 for men). These averages suggest the following:

1. The men and women differ as to which cognitive operations are most connected to life 40 years previously.
2. For women, cognitive and affective operations show the highest percentage of significant over time correlations, while self-reflective operations do for the men.

Percentage differences between different operations are not great, however, and argue for caution in their interpretation. The least these data suggest is that differentiations among the generalized constructs of coping, defense, and disorganization, while based upon sound theoretical reasoning and useful in other research designs, looses explanatory potency when the time unit under analysis covers 40 years of adult life. The "noises" of sample selection, measurement errors, and of course, 40 years of adult life experience reduce one's ability to see over time associations to particular, highly detailed behaviors.

Table 4. Average Number of Significant Antecedent Associations to
Four Ego Operations In Old Age

Ego operation[a]	Adaptability Defined as			
	Coping	Defense	Disorganization	Total
Women (n of 71)				
cognitive operations	14.3	12.0	8.3	11.0
self-reflective operations	4.7	8.7	12.0	8.4
attention-focusing operations	8.0	2.0	1.0	3.7
affective operations	12.0	7.7	16.0	12.0
Men (n of 24)				
cognitive operations	5.0	3.3	1.7	3.3
self-reflective operations	1.0	7.3	6.0	4.7
attention-focusing operations	5.0	2.0	2.0	3.0
affective operations	2.7	1.7	1.0	1.7

[a] For women there are 68 possible significant associations; for men, 50.

Rather, connections between larger and more encompassing units of behavior seem to provide the level on which long term, life course analysis can be made, at least for these data and this sample.

CONTEMPORARY DIFFERENCES BETWEEN HIGH COPERS, HIGH DEFENDERS, AND HIGH DISORGANIZED PARENTS

To what degree do contemporary aspects of intelligence, health, economics, personality, and family distinguish parents high on coping, or defense, or disorganization in old age? To pursue this question, distributions on the coping, defense, and disorganization summary measures were tricotomized. Parents who were in the highest third on one summary measure (but no other) were identified as copers, or defenders, or disorganized. Some parents were in the highest third on two summary measures and were excluded from this analysis.

T-tests, X^2, or Fisher's exact test contrasts were performed between all groups on a range of 41 measures selected from a larger pool of aging parents' study measures (see Maas and Kuypers, 1974). Measures were included which reflected status and behavior in the five areas previously used to determine early adult life antecedents of ego functioning and are listed in Table 5. Column entries in Table 5 indicate significant differences (and the direction of differences) between the coping, defensive, and disorganized groups. (No disorganized fathers could be identified, allowing only one father contrast—between high copers and high defenders.)

Inspection of Table 5 indicates the following:

1. Copers (either in contrast to defenders or disorganized parents and primarily for the mothers) show a pattern of high mental capacity, satisfactions with economic status, personal satisfactions, freshness and openness, and enjoyable marital relations. This pattern is most apparent when copers are contrasted with defenders (contrast 1).

2. Disorganized mothers (contrasts 2 and 3) are distinguished by aspects of self-assessed health (lower), satisfaction with finances (lower), and lack of family closeness (only in contrast to copers).

3. In contrast to the finding that early antecedents of ego functioning in old age relate most to intelligence, socioeconomics and family, the contemporary difference between levels of ego functioning cover all areas, with the exception of health.

These data suggest that aspects of intellectual performance, economics, and marital closeness relate to variations in ego functioning both early and late along the adult life course. Health status, surprisingly, is not related to ego functioning either early or late in adult life. Our sample of parents, as already noted, is relatively healthy. Stronger associations may have emerged between health and ego functioning if some of the parents were less physically intact. On the other hand, the personality correlates of ego functioning are more apparent late than early. They relate mostly to personal satisfaction and openness of interpersonal exchange and are apparent for both men and women.

DISCUSSION

The relative advantages (for late life ego development) of early adult life intellectual capacity and socioeconomic resources are indicated in this data. Although it is not clear that lower capacity or relative disadvantage is necessarily detrimental to ego development in late life, the eventual demonstration of superior levels of coping seems rooted in these two aspects of early adult life. They provide an argument for the degree to which successes in the ways of aging are contingent on certain potentials and environmental supports of earlier years. For the men in our sample, socioeconomic status emerged as the one most

Table 5. Contemporary Differences Between High Copers, High Defenders and High Disorganized Parents

Area and measure	Mothers' Contrasts[a,b]			Fathers
	I	II	III	IV
Intelligence (5 measures)				
estimated intellectual capacity	copers high[e]			
mental alertness	copers high[e]			
speed of mental process	copers high[d]			copers high[d]
accuracy of thinking	copers high[e]			
use of language	copers high[e]			
Age and Health (6 measures)				
age				
health (self-assessment)		copers positive[c]	def. pos[c]	
satisfaction with health				
involvement in sick role			def low[c]	
self-care difficulty				
energy output				
Socioeconomic and Work (5 measures)				
occupation status				
occupation stability				copers high[c]
involvement in past work				
economic status	copers high[c]	copers high[c]		
satisfaction with finances		copers high[e]	def high[e]	
Personality (12 measures)				
freshness	copers fresh[c]			
restlessness				
talkativeness				

128

Measure	I	II	III	IV
poise				
criticalness				
self-esteem				
cheerfulness				
worrisomeness				
excitability				
satisfaction	copers high[e]	copers high[c]		copers high[d]
openness	copers open[e]		def closed[e]	copers open[e]
frankness	copers frank[e]		disorg frank[c]	copers frank[d]

Marriage and Family (13 measures)

Measure	I	II	III	IV
marital status				
marital adjustment	copers high[e]			copers high[d]
interdependence in marriage				
closeness in marriage	copers close[d]			copers close[d]
instrumentality in marriage				
balance of decision making				
openness to spouse				
satisfaction in marriage	copers high[c]			
closeness to Child-S				
friendliness to Child-S	copers high[c]			copers friendly[c]
instrumentality with Child-S				
involvement as parent				

mothers

fathers

[a]
I   High copers (n = 15) vs. high defenders (n = 14)
II High copers (n = 21) vs. high disorganized (n = 9)
III High defenders (n = 14) vs. high disorganized (n = 11)
IV High copers (n = 17) vs. high defenders (n = 9)   —

[b] t-tests or X^2 statistics were used to contrast groups, except where d.f.'s were less than 21, in which case the Fisher's exact test was used.

[c] $p \leq .10$
[d] $p \leq .05$
[e] $p \leq .01$

important foundation for later ego capacity, suggesting the degree to which work related issues serve to pattern the tempo of adult development for males. Data on the intellectual potentials of the men are absent, however, and do not allow an assessment of whether the *combination* of socioeconomic advantage and intellectual capacity observed for women also holds for men. One might suspect so and the cautious reader is prompted to consider early intellectual capacities as equally important in the life course development of men, or at least until proven otherwise.

Ego failures (also related to the disadvantages of lower education and limited finances) seemed equally rooted in early adult life interpersonal tension and marital disharmony. Perhaps the trajectory of the development of ego disorganization is primarily founded on the stresses economic limitation impose *in combination* with the tensions a conflictual and distant interpersonal environment creates.

Observers of the etiology of mental illness actively debate the influence of biology, environment, social labeling, and zeitgest, among others, as explanations for the foundations of psychological failures, however defined, are searched. In this study, where failure was defined as ego disorganization, the critical impact of incompatible interpersonal relations seems to lend support to those who look to aspects of mutuality, bond, and harmony between people as the sources of mental disturbance. These data support E. Erikson's predictions that the intimacy tasks of early adulthood, if failed, forecast poorly the subsequent ego development in old age. These over time associations argue that one important foundation for the continued life course development of adaptability rests on the ability to relate to people, to find meaning in intimacy, and to experience the secure foundations of a social environment which provides warmth and closeness. These qualities, at the least, may reduce the probability of developing ego weakness later in life. Combined with capacities of mental alertness and accuracy and with advantages of educational training and economic support, the environment for the development of ego strengths may be provided.

It should not be overlooked in this study that over time associations between aspects of life covering 40 years of adulthood *were* indeed observed. Persons are rooted in previous ways of being, perhaps prisoners to some aspects and beneficiaries of others. Yet, the effects of social reorganizations, social withdrawals, physical losses, and mental changes of late life, often thought to produce change in the psychology of aging, must be counter-balanced with observations of the degree to which variations in old age are patterned by historical trajectories. Ego capacities certainly may be altered in old age, by encroaching social isolation or physical and mental deterioration, yet they seem also connected to aspects of life many years previously.

These observations suggest that preparations for and anticipations of what later life will provide must consider the entire adult life line. Failures of young marriages, frustrations in establishing and nurturing intimacy, and interpersonal hostilities of young adults should be looked to carefully for how they might forecast later development. Marital counseling and various techniques which seek to reduce interpersonal boundaries might well be supported for the long range impact their successes might have on how well people age.

It is at once comforting to observe that aging styles are not entirely contingent on old age related changes in physiology and social penetration (among many of the changes which often surround aging). Persons seem patterned by their own pasts and can maintain continuity through time in the face of often dramatic change. Yet it is also somewhat disconcerting, at least in the case of our more disorganized older persons, to observe connections reaching back to young adulthood. Are some persons "locked" onto a pattern of ego failure: patterns born from ways of relating and environmental resources quite early in adult life? And what are the possibilities of altering the degree to which certain persons may be "prisoners" of their past? These questions, and many more, promise to be explored as research into the historical roots of aging styles becomes more expanded. With more complete maps of various life courses, some which end in failure, some in success, critical factors and periods may be identified. So too, as the historical roots of various aging styles become known, persons can anticipate their own aging with a fuller understanding of cause and effect, of history and contemporaneous change.

Limitations of sample representativeness (the present sample is economically and physically advantaged), and inadequacies in measurement procedures of data collected 40 years ago must be kept in mind as one considers data presented. With greater variations in health, stronger associations to ego functioning might have been observed. Further, one must consider the level of focus of early personality measures—all minimally associated over time to old age adaptability. Wanda Bronson (1968) has argued that life course analysis of personality shows certain genotypic constancy *and* phenotypic variability. Behavior which on first examination appears to reflect change may, in terms of its organizational roots, be the changing overcoat of a more central unchanging core. One might suspect that the early measures of personality related to the more surface and situation-variable overcoat. More enduring personality characteristics which may relate to ego functioning in old age may have gone unnoticed as measured 40 years ago, in the early 1930's.

SUMMARY

Correlational analyses between 30 measures of ego functioning in old age and 68 measures of early adult life behavior (50 for men) on 95 persons (71 women and 24 men) revealed that aspects of adaptability in old age were associated to aspects of behavior 40 years previously, when the 70 year old parents of the 1970's were 30 years old and parents of infant children then being studied at the University of California. The strength of over time association varied according to 1) the sex of the subject (where stronger associations were observed for women than men), 2) the model of ego functioning used to define adaptability in old age (coping, defense, or disorganization), and 3) the specific area of early adulthood under consideration (intelligence, health, socioeconomic status, personality, and marital relations).

Early health status and personality were not related to later ego development and beg for further research to explain why. Aspects of intellectual capacity (and only for women where data on intelligence was available) and socioeconomic status (particularly education, lack of financial strain, high socioeconomic status, and high geographic mobility) related to adaptability defined as ego-coping behavior, a model which describes variations in ego strengths. When adaptability was described as variations in ego failures, a different pattern of early life associations was observed. In this case and especially for the women, socioeconomic disadvantages *and* conflictual and distant marital relations in young adulthood related to old age ego disorganization.

These data were taken to indicate the substantial impact aspects of young adulthood have on styles of aging, particularly ego functioning. Further, developmental assumptions as to the critical importance of establishing mutuality and intimacy in young adult life were supported, lending further support for therapies of various sorts which serve to reduce marital and interpersonal tension in young adulthood.

REFERENCES

Bronson, W. C. Stable patterns of behavior: The significance of enduring orientations for personality development. In J. P. Hill (Ed.), *Minnesota Symposium on Child Psychology*, Vol. 11. Minneapolis: University of Minnesota Press, 1968.

Block, J. in collaboration with Norma Haan *Lives Through Time*, Bancroft Books, Berkeley, 1971.

Erikson, E. H. *Childhood and society*. New York: W. W. Norton and Co., 1950.

Freud, A. *The ego and the mechanisms of defense*. New York: International Universities Press, 1966.

Haan, N. A tripartite model of ego functioning values and clinical research applications. *Journal of Nervous and Mental Disease*, 1969, 148, 14-30.

Havighurst, R.J. *Developmental tasks and education*. University of Chicago Press, 1949.

Jones, M. C., Bayley, N., Macfarlane, J. W., and Honzik, M. P. (Eds.) *The course of human development*. Waltham, Mass.: Zerox College Publishing, 1971.

Kuypers, J. Internal-external locus of control, ego functioning and personality characteristics in old age. *The Gerontologist*, Vol. 12, No. 2, Part I, Summer 1972.

Maas, H. and Kuypers, J. *From Thirty to Seventy: A Forty-year Longitudinal Study of Adult Life Styles and Personality*, Jossey-Bass, S. F., 1974.

Macfarlane, J. W. Studies in child guidance: I. Methodology of data collection and organization. *Monographs of The Society for Research in Child Development*. Vol. III, No. 6, Serial 19. Washington, D.C.: National Research Council, 1938.

Peck, R. *The psychology of character development*. New York: Wiley, 1960.

Smith, M. B. Competence and socialization. In Clausen, J. *Socialization and society*. Boston, Mass.: Little, Brown, 1968.

chapter 9

PATTERNS OF PERSONALITY DEVELOPMENT IN MIDDLE-AGED WOMEN: A LONGITUDINAL STUDY*

Florine B. Livson

Life expands at fifty—for non-traditional women who live traditional lives. More traditional women move smoothly into middle age with little change in life style. I will take a longitudinal look at personality development from adolescence to middle age in twenty-four women who had achieved a relatively high level of psychological health by age fifty—with special attention to changes in the middle adult years (ages 40 to 50).

The decade between ages forty and fifty, most investigators agree, brackets a critical transition in the life span, often punctuated by stress [1, 2, 3]. At forty most individuals are still engaged in tasks begun as young adults; at fifty a person is middle-aged. The decade of the forties brings a change in time perspective linked to a growing awareness of death as a personal reality [4]. As time perspective narrows, there is a tendency to turn inward, to reappraise one's self and one's goals. By the late forties and early fifties, however, this process tends to stabilize with a redefinition of goals and coming to terms with oneself [2, 3].

For women who are housewives and mothers, the transition into middle age is

* The data for this study are from the longitudinal Oakland Growth Study at the Institute of Human Development, University of California, Berkeley. Data collection was supported, in part, by the Ford Foundation, by National Institute of Mental Health Grant M-5300, and, most recently, by National Institute of Child Health and Development Grant HD-3617-06. The author is pleased to acknowledge her debt to the director and staff of the Institute of Human Development. This paper is drawn from the author's doctoral dissertation at the Wright Institute Graduate School, Berkeley, California. The paper was prepared while the author was a postdoctoral fellow supported by National Institute of Mental Health Grant MH08268 to the Department of Sociology, University of California, Berkeley.

usually linked to the departure of children and the biological changes of menopause. The post-parental years as a significant phase in a woman's life is a relatively new social phenomenon. With increased longevity—today a woman of forty-five will live on the average thirty-three more years—and with smaller families and the earlier departure of children, a woman can expect a longer period without her children than in earlier generations. The average woman today retires from mothering at forty-seven as compared with fifty-five at the end of the last century [5]. These writers point out that this is also the average age at menopause and the age when the number of women in the labor force rises most sharply.

How do the challenges of change at mid-life—social and biological—affect psychological well-being in women? Investigators do not agree. Medical and psychiatric literature abounds with accounts of the stresses of the climacteric and the so-called involutional disorders. Recent studies of healthy women in the community, however, question the generality of these observations. The departure of children—once the process of separation is completed—often leads to improved life satisfaction in the post-parental years [4, 6]. Menopause for many women is less stressful than commonly believed and postmenopausal women may even view this biological change as a positive event [6, 7]. Bart reports that in cultures in which women's social status rises in the middle years, menopause is not seen as stressful [8]. Neugarten observes that when major role losses in middle life are predictable and occur "on schedule" in the normal life course, they can be anticipated and worked through without disrupting the woman's sense of self [4].

Do role changes in the middle years allow some women not only to adapt but to expand their psychological horizons? Parts of the personality that were suppressed because they were not congruent with the roles of mother and young adult may surface to add new dimensions to the person. Does moving out of the mothering role, for example, allow a woman more flexibility in whether or not she conforms to traditional feminine sex roles? Chiriboga and Thurnher [6] report that sixty-year-old women view themselves as more assertive and effective than do women at fifty and Neugarten and Gutmann [9] find that women become more accepting of their aggressive impulses in the later years of life.

The present study describes two patterns of personality development leading to psychological health by age fifty in women who have been observed since adolescence. It explores differences between women whose personalities expand in the decade between forty and fifty and those who continue on more or less the same course throughout the middle years.

The twenty-four women in this study are drawn from a larger group of forty-two women who remained in the longitudinal Oakland Growth Study (Institute of Human Development, University of California, Berkeley) throughout adolescence (ages 11 to 18) and at *both* adult follow-ups (roughly ages 40 and 50).[1] They were selected on the basis of relatively high scores on an index of psychological health at age fifty (see below).

The California Q sort developed by Block was used to obtain personality profiles of participants at each of the four age periods studied : early and late adolescence, approximately ages forty and fifty [10, 11].[2] Q sorts at these four ages made it possible to assess personality changes over time and to estimate overall level of functioning, or "psychological health." The index of psychological health, developed by Livson and Peskin [12], was the correlation between each woman's Q sort and an "ideal" sort of a psychologically healthy person, representing a composite of sorts by four clinical psychologists.[3] The psychological health sort stresses qualities such as warm, giving, responsible, productive, insightful—and relatively free of neurotic signs. Psychological health scores are not related to intelligence or socioeconomic status and do not favor either sex.

Using this measure, I selected the healthiest members of the larger sample at age fifty for study: twenty-four women who scored above the mean on the index of psychological health. Two groups of healthy women were identified: seventeen whose health had *improved* from ages forty to fifty; and seven whose health had remained high and *stable* since forty.

Are these two groups, both psychologically healthy by age fifty, made up of women with different personality styles? Does each follow a different path of development toward this "end product" over the four age periods? I will contrast the two groups on the basis of significant personality (Q-sort) differences between them at each age level.[4] Though, for ease of exposition, each group will be described as a separate personality type, it should be kept in mind that these descriptions are relative one to the other.

[1] Participants in the Oakland Growth Study, which began in 1931-32 with over 200 boys and girls entering junior high school, were observed continuously throughout their junior and senior high school years and were interviewed again intensively in the late 1950s and 1960s. All were white. The forty-two women who remained in the study at all four age periods are (at age 50) predominantly middle-class housewives. Their average educational level is slightly beyond high school. They tend to be of slightly higher socioeconomic status than those who dropped out, better educated, and more effective socially. All but one married and have children. Average family size is between two and three children. The group, on the whole, is family-centered, though about half have part-time jobs and a few work full time. One-third have been divorced, but most are remarried. They are predominantly Protestant, urban, and financially comfortable.

[2] Each respondent was Q-sorted independently by at least two judges (clinically trained psychologists and psychiatric social workers) at each age period; judges had no access to data from other age periods. Mean interjudge reliabilities (computed by the Spearman-Brown prophecy formula) for Oakland Growth Study women ranged from .73 to .75.

[3] The reliability of the composite sort is .95, reflecting an average first-order interjudge agreement of .82.

[4] Differences reported at each age level are significant at least at the .10 level.

Traditionals and Independents

AGE FIFTY DIFFERENCES

The stable group at fifty are gregarious, nurturant women, pleased with their appearance, and conventional in their outlook. They place high value on closeness with others. They are seen as "feminine." I have called this group *traditionals*. Interviewers describe them as charming, cordial, generous, good hostesses. Their sociability is expressed in trusting, protective relations with others. Their defenses are of a hysterical type—anxiety is handled by repression and somatization—but their defenses work well. Overall, these are well-functioning, conforming women who are extroverted in that they turn outward for satisfaction. They rely on ego functions that further interpersonal skills. These qualities are well-suited to traditional roles of wife and mother—which may account for their high psychological health score at forty when their children were still dependent. These are women with minimal conflict between their personalities and social role.

Improvers present a different picture. These women at fifty are ambitious, skeptical, and unconventional in their way of looking at things. They rely on their intellect to cope with the world. I have labelled this group *independents*. Being verbal and expressive, they impress others as interesting people with high intellectual ability. (They do not in fact differ from traditionals in IQ as measured by the WAIS at age 50.) In brief, they are more autonomous than traditionals and more in touch with their inner life. They cope with conflicting feelings by insight and direct expression, rather than by conformity and repression. They are "doers," with interests in activities that are skill-oriented, rather than primarily social. Their main satisfactions come from developing their "selves," rather than attachment to others.

The two groups do not differ significantly in their demographic characteristics at fifty. Both are predominantly upper-middle class, financially comfortable, and Protestant. Their educational levels are similar—slightly beyond high school. Average family size of both groups is between two and three children, and average ages of children are comparable, ranging from nineteen to twenty-five. At least half of both groups still have some children living at home.

In their life styles at fifty, however, traditionals are more home-oriented. All are currently married and primarily housewives. One-third of independents are divorced or widowed and have full-time jobs.

PATTERNS OF DEVELOPMENT

How do traditionals and independents differ earlier in life? What path does each follow over the life span leading to psychological health by age fifty? I will trace the development of each group by describing personality differences between them at each age period. Both groups by early adolescence reveal a ground plan—a core characterological style—that evolves over the life span, roughly following Erikson's stages of adult development [13].

Traditionals — From early adolescence, traditionals are gregarious, feminine, conventional, and rely on repressive defenses. However, these key strategies in dealing with life are less fully formed than at later periods. Traditionals' gregariousness has not yet differentiated into the more subtle social skills observed later. There are signs of insecurity.

By late adolescence, they develop a more integrated, articulated style. These are popular, sociable young women in high school, successful in their femininity and perfecting their social skills. Signs of anxiety have dropped away. They are establishing, in Erikson's terms, ego identity.

By age forty, gregariousness remains their most prominent characteristic, but has now matured beyond the popularity of adolescence. They are close, trusting, and giving in their relationships with others. Poised and aware of the impression they create, they arouse liking. They have evolved a repertoire of skills that serve their core needs for sociability—and these needs themselves have matured, in the sense of becoming less narcissistic or self-oriented. They seem well into the stage of intimacy described by Erikson. The aging crisis of the forties described by many investigators does not seem to affect them.

By age fifty, traditionals have developed a protective attitude toward others. Their gregariousness, while remaining at a high level, has evolved beyond intimacy and trust into nurturance. Traditionals, by fifty, have moved into Erikson's middle adult stage of generativity. Their feminity is now clearly colored by this quality of protectiveness.

Independents — Like traditionals, independents reveal key personality traits in early adolescence that hold up to age fifty and organize their adult development. From early adolescence, independents value intellectual matters and are achievement-oriented, introspective, and unconventional. Like traditionals, however, they reveal signs of insecurity in this earlier period.

By late adolescence, independents achieve a more integrated level of functioning. Their intellectuality is now enriched by an interesting, arresting style. They now appear brighter than traditionals. (Again, there are no differences between groups in tests of actual ability.) The anxiety apparent earlier has eased off. They are developing a consistent, adaptive personality style.

By age forty the picture changes. Independents are depressed, irritable, conflicted. They no longer use their intellectuality in an adaptive way. Their originality and introspectiveness have turned to fantasy and daydreams. They seem out of touch with their intellectual interests and creative potential. Their overall psychological health score is relatively low. These women who seemed to be progressing toward a firm identity in adolescence appear to have regressed. They do not move into the stage of intimacy observed in traditionals by this age. Whether this regression is a brief transitional crisis around forty, or whether it was continuous throughout the adult years, I cannot say since Q sorts were not available for early adulthood. There is some retrospective evidence, however, that these women had higher morale in the early years of mothering when they could exercise their achievement skills in child-care.

This crisis is resolved by age fifty with a dramatic rebound in their intellectuality and a general freeing of emotional life. Intellectual skills that declined by forty again rise to prominence. By fifty, independents seem to revive the identities they were developing in adolescence. At the same time, closeness to others and trust increase. Independents are now giving, warm, sympathetic, and open in their feelings. Having settled the earlier issue of ego identity, these women by fifty move into the stage of intimacy achieved by forty in the traditional group.

Discussion

Both groups by fifty have evolved a "self" consistent with earlier characterological positions, but more differentiated and complex. Each, however, follows a different course with different timing. Traditionals show steady personality growth from adolescence to middle age. Independents interrupt their development in the middle adult years, but leap forward by fifty. I suggest that the key factor is the fit between a woman's life style and personality. Traditional personalities fit conventional feminine roles. As wives and mothers, they are able to live out valued aspects of themselves. They continue to find satisfaction in relationships with others, even as their children grow older and leave home. They are not motivated to change themselves or their situations at middle age.

> Mrs. T., typical of this group, has been married twenty-four years and is the mother of two daughters, both married and living in distant communities. She comments: "It seems like ever since they got married, we've been doing with the kids . . . Either they're running up here or we're running down there . . . Both girls come home at least a week a month . . . and then it takes me a couple of weeks to get over their visits because all their friends arrive."
>
> With others too, Mrs. T continues to find satisfaction in mothering and in ties with younger people and friends. "Our house is filled with people all the time. We entertain constantly . . . it seems there are eighteen cousins all my girls' age, that love us, and they're all married and having babies too now . . . And we have a lot of friends. And most of it isn't planned entertaining; it's just visits. They drop in."

Independents do not so easily fit conventional definitions of feminity. By age forty, when children are moving into adolescence, they seem to be confronted with an identity crisis. Having suppressed their intellectual competence and grown away from child-care skills, they seem unable for a time to connect with a workable identity. I would suggest that it is disengagement from the mothering role by fifty that stimulates these women to revive their more assertive goal-oriented skills. However, there is little evidence that independents directly reject or even resent their domestic life style while children are at home. Most were conscientious parents who internalized their roles as wives and mothers and homemakers.

Mrs. I, for example, experienced a transformation after the departure of her youngest child two years ago. Mrs. I had interrupted a promising career in the business world to marry when she was twenty-four. She is the mother of three children, two daughters and one son, now grown and living away from home. She was an able and devoted mother; but at the same time her life style seemed to bring out dependent, fearful qualities. She hesitated to ask her husband for money and was shy about going out alone. She became overweight, fatigued, and suffered from numerous health problems. When her youngest child left home, she became visibly depressed.

Searching for something to fill her time, she became involved with a charitable group. Hired by the organization as a receptionist, she has parlayed this job into a responsible administrative position and now plays a key role in its management. There has been a corresponding change in her outlook. She lost thirty pounds. Her health improved. She looks and feels attractive, enjoys buying clothes "like a teenager." Her marriage has become more equalitarian and more comfortable. Mrs. I has become an energetic, competent woman with high self-esteem—as though she was able to pick up the threads of her youth when she enjoyed an independent career.

The patterns described here do not, of course, exhaust all possible routes to psychological health at age fifty, even among housewives and mothers of this generation and social group. Neither do they reflect how prevalent these patterns are in the general population. They do illustrate two different but, in the end, successful paths a woman can take from adolescence to middle age if she is born at a time and place where traditional roles for women are part of her social world and are internalized in her expectations of herself. With changing social patterns, young women today have more options to choose life styles that suit them throughout their adult years.

The key factor seems to be the fit between a woman's life style and her personality. For women with a conventionally feminine orientation, traditional roles do not seem particularly restricting. For women who are less conventionally feminine—who prefer to deal with life in modes usually defined as masculine—traditional roles can be restricting. Such women may pay a serious price when they internalize traditional role expectations. But role expectations change at different life periods and in different social contexts. In many cultures, and to an extent in our own, recent evidence suggests that sex roles become less distinct and even converge in the second half of life [14]. Middle age can loosen the boundaries of one's life style and call forth suppressed parts of the self.

REFERENCES

1. E. Frenkel-Brunswik, Adjustments and Reorientation in the Course of the Life Span, In B. L. Neugarten (ed.), *Middle Age and Aging: A Reader in Social Psychology*, University of Chicago Press, Chicago, pp. 74-84, 1968.
2. R. L. Gould, The Phases of Adult Life: A Study in Developmental Psychology, *American Journal of Psychiatry, 129*:5, pp. 33-43, 1972.
3. D. J. Levinson, C. M. Darrow, E. B. Klein, M. Levinson and B. McKee, The Psychosocial Development of Men in Early Adulthood and the Mid-life Transition, In D. F. Ricks, A. Thomas and M. Ruff (eds.), *Life History Research in Psychopathology, 3,* University of Minnesota Press, Minneapolis, 1974.
4. B. L. Neugarten, Adaptation and the Life Cycle, *Journal of Geriatric Psychiatry, 4,* pp. 71-87, 1970.
5. B. L. Neugarten and J. W. Moore, The Changing Age-Status System, In B. L. Neugarten (ed.), *Middle Age and Aging: A Reader in Social Psychology*, University of Chicago Press, Chicago, pp. 22-28, 1968.
6. D. Chiriboga and M. Thurnher, Concept of Self, In M. Lowenthal, M. Thurnher, and D. Chiriboga, *Four Stages of Life*, Jossey-Bass, San Francisco, pp. 62-83, 1975.
7. B. L. Neugarten, V. Wood, R. J. Kraines and B. Loomis, Women's Attitudes Toward the Menopause, In B. L. Neugarten (ed.), *Middle Age and Aging: A Reader in Social Psychology*, University of Chicago Press, Chicago, pp. 195-200, 1968.
8. P. Bart, Depression in Middle-Aged Women, In V. Gornick and B. K. Moran (eds.), *Women in Sexist Society*, Basic Books, New York, pp. 163-186, 1971.
9. B. L. Neugarten and D. Gutmann, Age-Sex Roles and Personality in Middle Age: A Thematic Apperception Study, In B. L. Neugarten (ed.), *Middle Age and Aging: A Reader in Social Psychology*, University of Chicago Press, Chicago, pp. 77-84, 1968.
10. J. Block, *The Q-sort Method in Personality Assessment and Psychiatric Research*, Charles C. Thomas, Springfield, Ill., 1961.
11. J. Block, in collaboration with N. Haan, *Lives Through Time*, Bancroft Books, Berkeley, Calif., 1971.
12. N. Livson and H. Peskin, Prediction of Psychological Health in a Longitudinal Study, *Journal of Abnormal Psychology, 72,* pp. 509-518, 1967.
13. E. H. Erikson, *Childhood and Society*, W. W. Norton & Co., New York, 1950.
14. D. Gutmann, The Cross-Cultural Perspective: Notes Towards a Comparative Psychology of Aging, In J. Birren and K. W. Schaie (eds.), *Handbook of Aging Psychology*, Van Nostrand Reinhold, New York, in press.

chapter 10

AGE DIFFERENCES IN PERSONALITY STRUCTURE REVISITED: STUDIES IN VALIDITY, STABILITY, AND CHANGE*

Paul T. Costa, Jr., Ph.D. and
Robert R. McCrae, Ph.D.

Self-report, multivariate trait approaches to personality have been attacked on several sides. On the one hand, writers like Mischel complain of the low correlations between different measures of the same trait, and the apparent empirical instability of traits, which are conceptualized as enduring aspects of personality [1]. On the other hand, researchers like Neugarten, who have found evidence of personality change through interviews and projective tests, have generally found little meaningful change in self-report objective measures, and see them as being insensitive to important developmental changes [2].

The present paper reports three studies on stability and change in personality as measured by self-report instruments. It assumes that "personality" is not a monolithic structure, but an organization of several domains, some of which show predominantly stability while others may show change with normal aging. Provided that reliable instruments are used, and conceptually appropriate analyses are undertaken, neither of the criticisms mentioned need apply.

The line of research continued here began with an examination of the structure of the Cattell Sixteen Personality Factor Questionnaire (16PF) in three age groups. Cluster analyses of the scales for participants in the age ranges twenty-five to thirty-four, thirty-five to fifty-four, and fifty-five to eighty-two

*This collaborative research was conducted as part of the Normative Aging Study, Veterans Administration Outpatient Clinic, and the University of Massachusetts at Boston. Research supported in part by the Medical Research Service of the Veterans Administration (Normative Aging Study) and the Council for Tobacco Research – U.S.A., Inc., Grant #1085 (University of Massachusetts). Portions of this paper were presented as a part of the Symposium, "Age and Personality Structure: 'Hold' and 'No Hold' Dimensions of Personality," Annual Convention of the American Psychological Association, Chicago, Illinois, September, 1975; and at the Annual Meeting of the Gerontological Society, San Francisco, California, November, 1977.

showed three clusters in each group [3]. The first cluster, Anxiety, consisted of four scales relevant to the domain of emotionality, anxiety, or maladjustment; the second, Extraversion, of four scales related to sociability and sensation seeking; and the third, Openness, contained scales representing a domain of experiential style. The first two clusters were essentially replicated across all age groups, and thus demonstrated the stability of personality structure so often discovered in the self-report medium [4, 5]. The third cluster was a different grouping of scales in each cohort, and seemed to correspond to a domain of personality subject to change and development with age.

The present paper is an attempt to examine the validity of the cluster or factor interpretations offered in the earlier paper, and to consider data relevant to the stability or change of personality in these domains. To this end, construct validity evidence from several standard self-report instruments will be presented, together with longitudinal stability coefficients for the Anxiety and Introversion-Extraversion clusters. Longitudinal evidence on age differences in the structure of Openness to experience is presented which necessitates a revision of previous interpretations of this domain. Finally, data relating the perceptual cognitive style of field-dependence to the tendermindedness component of the third cluster will be presented to illustrate how experiential style may change with age.

Methods

PARTICIPANTS

Participants in this study were drawn from a population of male volunteers in the Normative Aging Study, a longitudinal study on normal health and aging [6]. Volunteers for the study were screened for physical and psychiatric health at time of entry, and for geographical stability. All but the lowest levels of socio-economic status are well-represented. For purposes of the present research, men were divided into three age groups: Young (N = 140, age range = 25-34), Middle (N = 711, age range = 35-54), and Old (N = 118, age range = 55-82). The number in different analyses varies, as data were not available for all men on all instruments; Ns are reported in the results tables.

MEASURES

Between September 1965 and November 1967, participants were administered forms A and B of the 1962 edition of the 16PF according to standard instructions [7]. On the same day they were given the General Aptitude Test Battery (GATB) [8] in small groups. Finally, they were given forms for the Allport-Vernon-Lindsay Scale of Values (AVL) and the Strong Vocational Interest Blank (SVIB) with instructions to fill them out at home and mail in.

Subsequent analyses of these measures lead to the identification of a small number of dimensions in each of wider generality than the many subscales of the original instruments. Factor analysis of the GATB [9] resulted in three dimensions labeled Information Processing Ability (IPA), Manual Dexterity (MD), and Pattern Analysis Capability (PAC). Five occupational interest factors were extracted from the SVIB [10] and identified as Person vs. Task Orientation; Theoretical vs. Practical Interaction Style; Toughmindedness vs. Tendermindedness; Self-Assertiveness vs. Retiring Altruism; and Business vs. Healing. The cluster analysis [11] of the 16PF resulted in the identification of the three personality domains mentioned above [3].

During the same period of time men taking their regular physical examinations filled out the Cornell Medical Index (CMI) [12] from which scores of Physical (sections A-L) and Psychiatric (sections M-R) complaints were obtained.

In two mailings in 1975 and 1976, participants received the A form of the 1967 edition of the Cattell 16PF and a short form of the Eysenck Personality Inventory (EPI-Q) measuring Neuroticism and Extraversion [13]. Cluster scores based on the 1975 information were calculated for these men from the 16PF scale scores. In a 1977 mailing items forming the I, M, and Q1 scales of the A form of the 1962 edition of the 16PF were administered as part of a larger questionnaire.

Finally, in 1975, as part of a small-scale study of hormones, ninety-four men selected for extremes of age within the group were given a battery of cognitive tests, individually administered, which included five Gottschalt Embedded Figures cards (EFT) and seven Wechsler Block Design cards. These were used as measures of field-independence.

Results and Discussion

STUDY 1: ANXIETY AND EXTRAVERSION

Cluster analyses in earlier work showed that the elements which compose these two clusters are stable over time. The present data confirm this view by showing a similar pattern of correlates for the two clusters in all three age groups. Tables 1 and 2 give the product moment correlations of Anxiety and Extraversion cluster scores with AVL, Strong factors, and CMI scales.

The extremely large N of the Middle group makes even trivial associations statistically significant, so an accurate understanding of these data require consideration of the size of the correlation as well as the significance level. Using .20 as the minimum value for a meaningful correlation, it can be seen that Anxiety shows few correlations with either values or occupational interests, the two exceptions being in the old group, where small negative correlations with Person vs. Task and Theoretical Style are observed. Since interests and values would not be expected to correlate with Anxiety, this provides evidence of discriminant validity. Anxiety does, however, correlate with psychiatric complaints on the CMI for all groups, and physical complaints for young and

Table 1. Correlations Between Anxiety Cluster and Strong Factors,
AVL Values, and CMI Portions for Three Age Groups

		Anxiety		
		Young (N = 128)	Middle (N = 678)	Old (N = 111)
AVL Values:	Theoretical	-09	-09	05
	Economic	-06	-10	14
	Aesthetic	-10	-03	07
	Social	13	11[b]	-09
	Political	18[a]	-01	-01
	Religious	-03	07[a]	-16[a]
		Young (N = 123)	Middle (N = 660)	Old (N = 105)
Strong Factors:	Person vs. Task	-00	-08[a]	-25[b]
	Theoretical Style	-11	-13[c]	-28[b]
	Tough-Mindedness	-05	-14[c]	-08
	Self-Assertiveness	-16[a]	-17[c]	-14
	Business vs. Healing	04	01	19[a]
		Young (N = 114)	Middle (N = 588)	Old (N = 84)
CMI Portions:	Physical Complaints	26[b]	34[c]	04
	Psychiatric Complaints	24[b]	42[c]	41[c]

NOTE: Decimal points omitted.
[a] p = .05.
[b] p = .01.
[c] p = .001.

middle groups. Both parts of the CMI have been shown to be related to neuroticism [14, 15].

Table 2 shows that, by contrast, Extraversion is unrelated to medical complaints but shows strong relations to occupational interests. In particular, the correlation of .60 with the Person vs. Task factor of the Strong SVIB is impressive evidence for the construct validity of the Extraversion cluster. The less strong but equally age-consistent correlations with Self-Assertiveness reflect the component of dominance and adventurousness which has generally been found to be an element of extraversion. Among older men, preference for healing over business is also characteristic of extraversion. Political (or power) values are associated with extraversion among the youngest group while social

Table 2. Correlations Between Extraversion Cluster and Strong Factors, AVL Values, and CMI Portions for Three Age Groups

		Extraversion		
		Young (N = 128)	Middle (N = 678)	Old (N = 111)
AVL Values:	Theoretical	-07	-18^c	-13
	Economic	-06	02	-09
	Aesthetic	-12	-11^b	-04
	Social	13	10^b	20^a
	Political	26^c	18^c	06
	Religious	-08	00	03
		Young (N = 123)	Middle (N = 660)	Old (N = 105)
Strong Factors:	Person vs. Task	63^c	61^c	67^c
	Theoretical Style	-05	-04	02
	Tough-Mindedness	-08	05	-09
	Self-Assertiveness	33^c	28^c	35^c
	Business vs. Healing	-18^a	-05	-28^b
		Young (N = 114)	Middle (N = 588)	Old (N = 84)
CMI Portions:	Physical Complaints	-01	-07^a	-14
	Psychiatric Complaints	-15	-12^b	-06

NOTE: Decimal points omitted.
^{a} p = .05.
^{b} p = .01.
^{c} p = .001.

(or humanitarian) values reach a correlation of .20 with extraversion among old men. This shift in emphasis from the dominance to the affiliative side of extraversion with age may be evidence of age changes in trait expression even within a structurally invariant domain.

A second line of evidence for stability in affective and interpersonal domains comes from an examination of longitudinal data. Table 3 presents the intercorrelations of Anxiety and Extraversion cluster scores from 1966, from the readministration of Form A of the 16PF in 1975, and from the EPI-Q, mailed to participants in 1976. Correlations between the Cattell measures over a nine-year period range from a low of .579 between measures of anxiety in the young group to a high of .838 between extraversion measures for the old group. Ten-year stability coefficients from the brief, and thus somewhat unreliable, Eysenck

Table 3. Intercorrelations of 1966 and 1976 Anxiety and Extraversion Cluster Scores and EPI-Q Extraversion and Neuroticism Scale for Three Age Groups (N in parenthesis)

	1.	2.	3.	4.	5.	6.
	Young					
1. 1966 Anxiety						
2. 1976 Anxiety	578^c (68)					
3. EPI-Q Neuroticism	406^c (113)	547^c (63)				
4. 1966 Extraversion	−143^b (140)	−074 (68)	001 (113)			
5. 1976 Extraversion	−041 (68)	−009 (68)	081 (63)	753^c (68)		
6. EPI-Q Extraversion	−265^b (113)	−292^c (63)	−260^c (129)	455^c (113)	630^c (63)	
	Middle					
1. 1966 Anxiety						
2. 1976 Anxiety	674^c (274)					
3. EPI-Q Neuroticism	493^c (585)	603^c (264)				
4. 1966 Extraversion	−210^c (711)	−109^a (274)	−161^c (585)			
5. 1976 Extraversion	−166^b (274)	−182^c (234)	−196^c (264)	700^c (274)		
6. EPI-Q Extraversion	−191^c (594)	−190^c (267)	−361^c (656)	543^c (594)	569^c (267)	
	Old					
1. 1966 Anxiety						
2. 1976 Anxiety	692^c (82)					
3. EPI-Q Neuroticism	542^c (87)	533^c (72)				
4. 1966 Extraversion	−200^a (116)	−110 (82)	−071 (87)			
5. 1976 Extraversion	−276^b (82)	−260^b (82)	−128 (72)	838^c (82)		
6. EPI-Q Extraversion	−227^a (88)	−149 (72)	−340^c (107)	528^c (88)	493^c (72)	

NOTE: Decimal points omitted. ^{a} p = .05. ^{b} p = .01. ^{c} p = .001.

measures of similar constructs range from .406 (again among the young for anxiety) to .543 (for extraversion among middle-aged men).

These are remarkably high correlations, equal to the re-test reliability coefficients of many personality tests. Retest values with the Cattell instruments would presumably have been even higher if identical forms (using both A and B forms of 1962 edition) had been obtained at the second administration. To the extent that self-report instruments provide accurate pictures of personality, it seems clear that personality is quite stable within these two domains. The evidence of cross-sectional consistency in internal structure and external correlates completes the picture of enduring organizations in these aspects of personality.

STUDY 2: AGE DIFFERENCES IN OPENNESS: A LONGITUDINAL RECONSIDERATION

The third domain identified by cluster analysis in the 16PF was originally found to be different in composition across three age cohorts. Among the young group, twenty-five to thirty-four, the cluster was composed of I, Tenderminded-ness, and M, Imaginativeness, and was interpreted as a dimension of openness to feelings and aesthetic experiences. For men thirty-five to fifty-four, I was replaced by Q1, Liberal Thinking, and the cluster took on the significance of openness to new ideas and values. In the oldest group, from fifty-five to eighty-two, both I and Q1 clustered together with M, as did B, Intellectual Brightness. An earlier interpretation [3] stressed the balancing of affect and aesthetic sensitivity with new ways of thinking and valuing in older men.

While an attempt to rule out the possibility of statistical artifact was made by replicating cluster differences in two repartitionings of the sample, it was recognized that such subtle changes required further verification, and that longitudinal data was needed to determine whether the effect, if real, was developmental or simply a cohort effect.

An attempt at a longitudinal verification using data from the 1967 edition of the 16PF (administered to participants in 1975) proved untenable, since the relevant scales had been almost completely rewritten in the later edition and their empirical relation to earlier forms of the scales was unknown. Consequently, the original items from the A form scales I, M, and Q1 were readministered to participants in 1977. Table 4 presents the correlations of these A-Form scales in the sub-sample tested in both 1966 and 1977 within the original age groups. Results are disconcerting: not only are the cluster differences not evident eleven years later, they are also not seen in the original data when only the A form is analyzed. Within the A form a simple IM cluster can be seen as the only relatively constant finding. Variations in the original cluster analysis on combined A and B forms appears to have been largely the result of error due to the unreliability of 16PF scales. The three age specific clusters should apparently be regarded not as successive phases in a developmental sequence but as a series of crude approxima-tions to an underlying, age-invariant dimension of Openness.

Table 4. Intercorrelations of 16PF A Form Openness Scales, in 1966 (Above Diagonal) and 1977 (Below Diagonal)

	B (Brightness)	I (Tendermindedness)	M (Imaginativeness)	Q1 (Liberal Thinking)
			Young (N = 56)	
B		-02	13	26[a]
I	-		24[a]	-25[a]
M	-	-11		10
Q1	-	20	-11	
			Middle (N = 286)	
B		06	14[b]	11[a]
I	-		29[c]	-04
M	-	35[c]		08
Q1	-	-13[a]	11[a]	
			Old (N = 60)	
B		-01	-07	01
I	-		21[a]	-06
M	-	29[a]		05
Q1	-	08	15	

NOTE: Decimal points omitted.
[a] p = .05.
[b] p = .01.
[c] p = .001.

Evidence that there is indeed a meaningful dimension underlying the third cluster can be seen in the pattern of external correlates of the overall cluster. In an analysis of the relations between personality dimensions and cognitive ability factors [9], a score for all participants regardless of age, was calculated by summing standard scores on scales M, Imaginativeness, and Q1, Liberal Thinking, since these two scales formed the third cluster when analysis was performed on the total group. This cluster score can be regarded as a rough measure of general openness to experience. Table 5 gives the correlations of the MQ1 cluster scores with other measures.

From this table it can be seen that openness is associated with the Theoretical Interaction Style factor of vocational interests, and with several values from the AVL. Theoretical and esthetic values are positively related to openness in all three groups, while economic and religious values, which can be interpreted as, at least in part, practical and authoritarian, are negatively related. These external correlates support the interpretation of the third cluster as a measure of

Table 5. Correlations Between Openness Cluster (M-Q1) and Strong Factors, AVL Values, and CMI Portions for Three Age Groups

		Openness		
		Young (N = 128)	Middle (N = 678)	Old (N = 111)
AVL Values:	Theoretical	29^c	21^c	26^c
	Economic	-34^c	-18^c	-38^c
	Aesthetic	38^c	23^c	29^c
	Social	04	-01	15
	Political	-21^b	-08^a	-11
	Religious	-17^a	-15^c	-17^a
		Young (N = 123)	Middle (N = 660)	Old (N = 105)
Strong Factors:	Person vs. Task	-21^b	-11^b	-08
	Theoretical Style	45^c	40^c	43^c
	Tough-Mindedness	-13	-17^c	-28^b
	Self-Assertiveness	03	-05	21^a
	Business vs. Healing	-06	-05	-15
		Young (N = 114)	Middle (N = 588)	Old (N = 84)
CMI Portions:	Physical Complaints	-13	03	-05
	Psychiatric Complaints	-02	01	-07

NOTE: Decimal points omitted.
^{a} p = .05.
^{b} p = .01.
^{c} p = .001.

experiential openness. Open individuals show intellectual curiosity and appreciation for art and beauty: for them experience is intrinsically interesting. Conceptually, at least, closed men have a pragmatic and dogmatic attitude toward experience, interpreting the world narrowly in terms of their values and needs. These differences are seen again in the contrast of occupational interest scales marking the Theoretical Interaction Style factor of the Strong: Open men share interests with Psychologists and Ministers; Closed men resemble Bankers and Morticians.

Further evidence for the interpretation of the third cluster as a dimension of openness is seen in its relation to a new instrument specifically designed to measure openness to various facets of experience [16]. While the failure to replicate age differences in personality structure is disappointing, the original cluster analysis must be credited with calling attention to this neglected and important dimension of personality.

STUDY 3: AGE DIFFERENCES IN PERSONALITY AND COGNITIVE STYLE

Despite the failure of the dimension of Openness to show longitudinal changes in personality structure, the idea of looking for changes in the relation between variables across age groups, instead of simple level changes, is too promising an approach to abandon. It is clear that there *are* developmental changes in the organization of personality, at least at the early stages of development. Stable dimensions of individual difference in conscientiousness, conformity, or political liberalism are not found in neonates and so must be the products of development. Post-maturational changes in personality organization, if they exist, can only be found through structural or qualitative approaches. If old adults are really different from young, and not simply more introverted or rigid or calm, then the differences must be in the nature of and relation between psychological variables.

With this rationale, the apparent changes in the third cluster led to a systematic search for changing relations between traits in the experiential domain. The result was the identification of a pair of variables which did show such a change across age groups: tendermindedness and field-dependence. With keen awareness of the fact that such apparent changes or differences may be spurious, we have chosen to report this finding as a promising beginning for future research.

In an extensive program of research, Witkin and his co-workers have shown that performance on disembedding tasks reflects not only a particular kind of intellectual competence, but also a highly generalized way of dealing with the environment [17, 18]. The cognitive style of field-independence is assessed by the ability to find hidden figures (or by other tasks), but it is related to occupational interests, cognitive complexity, and even forms of psychopathology. Witkin has interpreted the underlying dimension as one of global vs. articulated approaches to experience.

Studies using a variety of operationalizations of field-dependence have generally concurred in finding that field independence is higher in young adults (as opposed to both children and older adults) [19]; in males [20]; and, within sexes, in more "masculine" individuals, as measured by traditional scales of masculinity-femininity [21]. Since tendermindedness is one of the traits most often identified as differentiating the sexes, it could be expected to follow this same pattern.

For a small sub-sample who had participated in another study within the Normative Aging Study, three measures of field-dependence were available: the EFT, Block Design, and Pattern Analysis Capability (PAC) factor of the GATB. The first two measures are more traditional and direct indices of field-independence, but the PAC factor, while less directly measuring field-independence, gives an opportunity to assess longitudinal stability and to validate results on a much larger sample. Tendermindedness is measured here by three scales: the 16PF I scales from 1966 and 1975 administrations, and the third factor of the SVIB, on which the Strong M-F scale has its chief loading. The Strong factor is derived from measures administered around 1966.

Table 6 presents the intercorrelations of these six measures for young (above the diagonal) and old (below the diagonal) groups. The correlations between the three alternative measures of each construct within each group provide evidence for the construct validity of each; and, since a nine-year interval separates one of the measures of each construct from the others, evidence of considerable longitudinal stability for both these traits.

An examination of the correlations between the two constructs shows a striking age difference: among the young men, seven of the nine correlations are significant, and all point to the previously reported finding of higher field-independence among more "masculine" persons. Among the old group, however, there are no significant correlations, and some show trends in the opposite direction.

Because of the smallness of the sample size there was concern for the

Table 6. Intercorrelations of Measures of Tendermindedness and Field-Dependence for Young (Above Diagonal) and Old (Below Diagonal) Men (Ns in parenthesis)

	1.	2.	3.	4.	5.	6.
1. Pattern Analysis Capability (Score Reflected)		67^b (16)	92^c (16)	28^c (148)	17^a (163)	30^b (68)
2. Embedded Figures Test Latencies	34^a (25)		69^c (45)	65^b (15)	44^a (15)	72^b (10)
3. Block Design Latencies	33 (25)	54^c (49)		36 (15)	28 (15)	65^a (10)
4. Strong Tough-Minded Factor (Reflected)	10 (129)	-02 (23)	04 (23)		56^c (143)	63^c (65)
5. 1966 "I" Scale	06 (144)	00 (25)	10 (25)	61^c (128)		55^c (68)
6. 1976 "I" Scale	06 (82)	-06 (21)	34 (34)	49 (77)	36^c (82)	

NOTE: Decimal points omitted.
[a] $p = .05$.
[b] $p = .01$.
[c] $p = .001$.

replicability of these findings. However, it was possible to consider large numbers of participants over a full age range by using the PAC measure. Table 7 gives the correlations between the three measures of toughmindedness and PAC scores for six age cohorts. In general, the pattern seems clear; with age, toughmindedness, or masculine traits and interests, becomes increasingly independent of the cognitive style of field-independence.

Despite the small size of several sub-samples and the statistical complications which arise from the fact that both field-dependence and tendermindedness change in level with age, there is considerable evidence here for the reality of a difference in the relation between these two variables across age groups (although, of course, the present data do not demonstrate that the differences are the result of longitudinal change). The associations reported are based on the correlations of self-report with performance measures, and thus are not likely to represent artifacts of method variance; they are replicated on multiple measures of both constructs, and on measurements taken nine years apart.

In addition, it is possible to interpret the results as being consistent with a growing body of research which points to the importance of changing sex-role identification in the later half of the life span [22–24]. According to this interpretation, in youth, when sex roles are most salient, they appear to

Table 7. Correlations of Pattern Analysis Capability with Tough-Mindedness for Six Age Groups (Ns in parenthesis)

Age in 1966	Strong Tough-Minded Factor	1966 "I" Scale (Reflected)	1976 "I" Scale (Reflected)
25–35	28[c] (148)	17[a] (163)	30[b] (68)
35–39	12[a] (203)	11 (221)	24[a] (71)
40–44	17[b] (215)	07 (222)	-03 (78)
45–49	16[a] (185)	14[a] (198)	16 (75)
50–54	13[a] (155)	15[a] (162)	18 (50)
55–82	10 (129)	06 (144)	06 (82)

NOTE: Decimal points omitted.
[a] p = .05.
[b] p = .01.
[c] p = .001.

dominate the organization of personality traits, interests, and cognitive styles. In adapting to the age-related expectations of young adulthood, men with high perceptual analytic abilities develop scientific, logical, objective, and impersonal attitudes and interests, while those with low analytic abilities adopt a more passive, subjective, emotional mode of adaptation. Throughout adulthood, this stereotypic configuration begins to break down. Sex-role differentiation between the sexes is known to moderate with age [22–24]; the present data suggest that a similar process occurs within the male sex. In the oldest men, thinking no longer precludes feeling, and field-independence is no longer the exclusive property of the toughminded. This general progression from social and role-dictated modes of experiencing to increasingly personalized and integrated styles may represent some form of the process of individuation.

The twin criticisms that self-report personality measures are too unstable to represent enduring consistencies in behavior and too insensitive to detect personality change can be evaluated in the light of the evidence presented here. Clearly, the first charge is not supported. Ample evidence is reported for meaningful dimensions of personality which show impressive stability over a nine-year interval in adults. While the evidence in the present paper is within the self-report medium and thus does not directly address the question of the relation between traits and observable behaviors, it argues at the least for an enduring and internally consistent self-image.

Demonstrating sensitivity to developmental changes is more difficult, and can most easily be done in the context of attempting to test specific hypotheses on personality changes with age. Nevertheless, the differing relation of tender-mindedness and field-dependence in young and old groups suggests that objective measures of personality can detect changes in those parts of personality where change is likely to occur.

REFERENCES

1. W. Mischel, *Personality and Assessment*, Wiley, New York, 1968.
2. B. L. Neugarten, *Personality in Middle and Late Life*, Atherton, New York, 1964.
3. P. T. Costa, Jr. and R. R. McCrae, Age Differences in Personality Structure: A Cluster Analytic Approach, *Journal of Gerontology, 31*, pp. 564-570, 1976.
4. J. H. Britton and J. O. Britton, *Personality Changes in Aging*, Springer, New York, 1972.
5. K. W. Schaie and F. A. Parham, Stability of Adult Personality Traits: Fact or Fable?, *Journal of Personality and Social Psychology, 34*, pp. 146-158, 1976.
6. B. Bell, C. L. Rose, and A. Damon, The Normative Aging Study: An Interdisciplinary and Longitudinal Study of Health and Aging, *Aging and Human Development, 3*, pp. 5-17, 1972.

7. R. B. Cattell, H. W. Eber, and M. M. Tatsuoka, *Handbook for the Sixteen Personality Factor Questionnaire,* Institute for Personality and Ability Testing, Champaign, Illinois, 1970.
8. United States Department of Labor, Division of Employment Security, *Manual for the Use of the General Aptitude Test Battery, Section III. Development,* U. S. Government Printing Office, Washington, D. C., 1967.
9. P. T. Costa, Jr., J. L. Fozard, R. R. McCrae, and R. Bosse, Relations of Age and Personality to Cognitive Ability Factors, *Journal of Gerontology, 31,* pp. 663-669, 1976.
10. P. T. Costa, Jr., J. L. Fozard, and R. R. McCrae, Personological Interpretation of Factors from the Strong Vocational Interest Blank Scales, *Journal of Vocational Behavior, 10,* pp. 231-243, 1977.
11. R. C. Tryon and D. E. Bailey, *Cluster Analysis,* McGraw-Hill, New York, 1970.
12. K. Brodman, A. J. Erdmann, Jr., I. Lorge, and H. G. Wolff, The Cornell Medical Index: An Adjunct to Medical Interview, *Journal of the American Medical Association, 140,* pp. 530-534, 1949.
13. B. Floderus, Psycho-Social Factors in Relation to Coronary Heart Disease and Associated Risk Factors, *Nordisk Hygienisk Tid Skrift Supplementum, 6,* Stockholm, Sweden, 1974.
14. A. Verghese, Relationships Between the Eysenck Personality Inventory N Score, the Cornell Medical Index M-R Score, and the Psychogalvanic Response, *British Journal of Psychiatry, 116,* pp. 27-32, 1970.
15. A. Ryle and M. Hamilton, Neurosis in 50 Married Couples, *Journal of Mental Science, 108,* p. 265, 1962.
16. P. T. Costa, Jr. and R. R. McCrae, Objective Personality Assessment, in M. Storandt, I. Siegler, and M. Elias (eds.), *Clinical Psychology in Gerontology,* Plenum, New York, in press.
17. H. A. Witkin, R. B. Dyk, H. F. Faterson, D. R. Goodenough, and S. A. Karp, *Psychological Differentiation,* Wiley, New York, 1962.
18. H. A. Witkin, P. K. Oltman, P. W. Cox, E. Erlichman, R. M. Hamm, and R. W. Rongler, *Field-Dependence-Independence and Psychological Differentiation,* Educational Testing Service, Princeton, New Jersey, 1973.
19. D. W. Schwartz and S. A. Karp, Field Dependence in a Geriatric Population, *Perceptual and Motor Skills, 24,* pp. 495-504, 1967.
20. M. Fiebert, Sex Differences in Cognitive Style, *Perceptual and Motor Skills, 24,* pp. 1277-1278, 1967.
21. J. Arbuthnot, Sex, Sex-role Identity, and Cognitive Style, *Perceptual and Motor Skills, 41,* pp. 435-440, 1975.
22. F. Livson, Sex Differences in Personality Development in the Middle Adult Years: A Longitudinal Study, Paper presented at 28th Annual Convention, Gerontological Society, Louisville, Kentucky, October 1975.
23. B. L. Neugarten, and D. L. Gutmann, Age-Sex Roles and Personality in Middle Age: A Thematic Apperception Study, *Psychological Monographs, 72,* (whole no. 470), 1958.
24. D. L. Gutmann, Female Ego Styles and Generational Conflict, in J. M. Bardwick, E. Douvan, M. S. Horner, and D. L. Gutmann (eds.), *Feminine Personality and Conflict,* Brooks/Cole, Belmont, California, 1970.